THE CONCEPTS
OF
COMPARATIVE
POLITICS

THE CONCEPTS
OF
COMPARATIVE
POLITICS

Martin C. Needler

PRAEGER

New York
Westport, Connecticut
London

Library of Congress Cataloging-in-Publication Data

Needler, Martin C.
    The concepts of comparative politics / Martin C. Needler.
       p.   cm.
    Includes bibliographical references and index.
    ISBN 0–275–93652–X. — ISBN 0–275–93653–8 (pbk.)
    1. Comparative government.   I. Title.
JF51.N44   1991
320.3—dc20   90–43159

British Library Cataloguing in Publication Data is available.

Library of Congress Catalog Card Number: 90–43159
ISBN: 0–275–93652–X (hb.)
      0–275–93653–8 (pbk.)

First published in 1991

Praeger Publishers, One Madison Avenue, New York, NY 10010
An imprint of Greenwood Publishing Group, Inc.

Printed in the United States of America

The paper used in this book complies with the
Permanent Paper Standard issued by the National
Information Standards Organization (Z39.48–1984).

10 9 8 7 6 5 4 3 2

To
THE MEMORY OF
CARL J. FRIEDRICH

CONTENTS

INTRODUCTION

I

The approach used here in the critique of concepts of comparative politics is analytical but also empirical. That is, the terms and concepts examined are discussed not only in terms of their internal logic and of the differing views of various writers but also of their adequacy in organizing experience of the "real world." The elaboration of theory should be a process of interactive iteration between theory and experience.

Thus, for example, a theory of political development may begin with a model of societies changing from a "traditional" character through one of "transition" to one of "modernity"; one may then construct an ideal type of a traditional society, in which, let us say, political roles are undifferentiated and modes of economic activity are unchanging. In fact, the literature abounds in such models. However, one should then decide which societies appear to fall into the "traditional" category, and conduct a more detailed examination of them. Such an examination may reveal (as it no doubt would) that in such societies political roles are highly differentiated and modes of economic activity do change. One should then treat the original description of the ideal type of traditional society as only a first approximation and revise it, perhaps abandoning the "undifferentiated roles" feature as nonessential to the character of a traditional society, and redefining the economic change variable to say that in traditional societies economic change does occur, but only slowly and intermittently.

It is of the greatest importance that the terms and concepts to be used in the construction of general theory correspond closely to the empirical entities to which they refer, since traits imputed to the theoretical type will generally be assumed to characterize the actual cases placed in the category described by the term. Thus, for example, it has become generally accepted to describe a totalitarian state as one in which the government has total control of communications, a monopoly of force, an official fixed ideology, and so on, and to place the Soviet Union in the category of totalitarian state. When evidence arrives that in fact the government does not have a monopoly of communications in the Soviet Union or that there are divisions in the leadership, or that some change is taking place, there are far too many people ready to deny the validity of the new evidence on the premise that in a totalitarian state such things are not possible and we know that the Soviet Union is a totalitarian state. We should always remember that while a term may be defined, an empirical reality can only be described. One must always be open to new evidence; the possibilities of an actually existent entity cannot be circumscribed by characteristics of the theoretical category in which it has been placed.

This problem is unfortunately widespread in the social sciences and presents a host of difficulties. One creates an ideal type and then proceeds to act as though some actually existent entity were a perfect reflection of the ideal type; or, in a sort of Platonic fallacy, one acts as though the ideal type represented the truest reality and the actual entity were no more than an imperfect copy of it. We should analyze things as they are and develop concepts and models as close as possible to the actual, rather than pretend that the actual embodies the ideal.

We need concepts. We need models, we need bodies of theory that will help us to understand the world. But the effort must be unrelenting to infuse theory with empirical content, to modify our concepts in the light of new data, to have the causal model approximate the process that goes forward in the real world.

II

The concepts used in political analysis, and the theories out of which they grow and to which they refer, must then be evaluated in terms of their own logic, their usefulness, and their correspondence to empirical reality. How well they stand up to examination by these criteria should be the only test of their acceptability; nevertheless, it is also of interest, and may be a valuable aid to understanding, to appreciate the manner in which the concept or theory developed in its intellectual, historical, and even political context. Such an understanding can constitute a contribution to the history of ideas or to the sociology of knowledge. Ideas do not spring fully formed from the thinker's brow, after all, but have a history of their own, and thus can be understood genetically as well as logically. It can thus be fair to comment, apropos of the development theory discussed above, for example, that the stereotyped model of "traditional" society one encounters in the literature suggests that writers in the field lack familiarity with such societies; or, similarly, the idea met with in the literature on totalitarianism, that full totalitarianism is only possible with modern technology, could only have been written by someone who had never lived in a Third World village.

If it is true that cultural, class-based, or political prejudices influence the development of a theoretical model, it may also be true that the adoption of a particular theoretical model has political repercussions.

This will appear from what follows. A model is at best a schematized abstraction from reality, dependent for its predictive value on simplification and the making of a series of assumptions. Dangers arise if one forgets that the assumptions may not actually all hold true in specific cases—in fact, are rarely likely to hold true completely. For example, there is a normative model of correct driving behavior, involving driving on the righthand side of the road, signaling turns, making right turns from the right lane and and left turns from the left lane, and so on. For this to become a predictive model describing expected behavior, however, assumptions need to be made about the knowledge, competence, and sobriety of other drivers. If one forgets that these are assumptions that may not always hold, an accident may result.

The consequences are particularly significant for economic models. Economists have at their disposal a powerful tool for analyzing behavior, predicting it, and making policy recommendations, in the competitive model of the economy. The model is both descriptive and normative: Given certain assumptions about information, motivation, and rationality, then if governments allow free economic activity, the result is the maximization of production and welfare. Free economic activity results, as though guided by an invisible hand, in the greatest well-being for the greatest number (leaving aside for the moment the problems associated with the existence of "externalities" and collective goods, the benefits of which cannot be pursued, and the costs of which cannot be borne, individually but only jointly.) Regrettably, however, economists are all too prone to take it for granted that the assumptions of the model hold when in fact they don't.

In recent years we have even been treated to the spectacle of authoritarian governments, such as that of General Pinochet in Chile, trying to impose the assumptions of the model by force; the invisible hand becomes the all-too-visible fist, as it were. Even in that case—apart from other theoretical and practical errors, such as the mismanagement of exchange rates— Pinochet's economists found that the forcible imposition of the model meant that exceptions to the working of the model had to be made for those whose collaboration was necessary for that imposition. That is, the military refused to have its budget cut and foreign banks refused to accept their losses on bad investments, no matter what the model said should occur. The curious irony is that in defending themselves against the criticisms to which the subsequent collapse of the Chilean economy gave rise, the economists typically protested that it was not their prescriptions but rather political factors that had caused the disaster. That is, in effect, they criticized reality because it failed to embody the assumptions of the model, rather than accepting that it was inappropriate to try to apply the model when the assumptions on which it was based did not hold in reality.

Often a particular model of reality becomes elaborated into a full-blown ideology. Although there are various technical definitions of ideology, in common parlance a political ideology embodies a particular descriptive understanding of the world, together with a prescription for desirable political outcomes. In politics there are two dangers: too much ideological thinking, and too little. This is illustrated by comparing the performance of—at the time of writing—the last two U.S. presidents, Ronald Reagan and Jimmy Carter. Reagan, the ideologist, refused to accept the existence of facts that questioned his view of the world. Carter became absorbed in questions of detail and failed to impose a single unifying vision on his presidency.

One must have a unifying vision, an integrated view of the world, which otherwise becomes a chaos of unintelligible events. However, possession of such a world-view should not be carried to the point of limiting one's ability to perceive factual situations correctly. Truth is not an absolute given for all time, much less the property of a single sect or school of thought. One's understanding of the world must be subject to continuous revision, as each new day contributes its input of raw data. This process of learning, this ever-closer approximation to the apprehension of truth, is an obligation that lasts as long as life itself.

I

CRISIS AND DISCONTINUITY

1

REVOLUTION

I

The term "revolution" fuses two concepts. One of these is the
idea of the seizure of political power by illegal means, that is,
by means not contemplated in the existing political system.
The other is that of a fundamental or thoroughgoing change
in the structure of society. When an event displays both of these
characteristics, there is no dispute that it is in fact a revolution.
Thus, for example, the French Revolution of 1789 substituted
a republic for the preexisting monarchy, going so far as to
behead the monarch. It also changed the regulations governing
society and the economy, abolishing feudal dues and rights and
attempting to reorder social and economic relations on the basis
of rationality, equality, and individual freedom. The Russian
Revolution of 1917 also led to the execution of the monarch
and the establishment of a republic, together with far-reaching
changes in property relations. Commentators typically make
a point of distinguishing from occurrences of this type those
that exhibited only one aspect of the definition of revolution.
That is, if power is seized illegally but the resulting regime

does not make fundamental changes, observers may say that this is a palace revolt but not a real revolution. On the other hand, a thoroughgoing change in some aspects of society that occurs without an irregular shift in political control may be referred to as a "peaceful revolution"—for example, a long-range shift in class relations or economic power brought about by a technological change or a change in the pattern of land use.

Other secondary connotations are attached to the idea of revolution. The violence that attends the seizure of power by a new group may be extended in time and among the population at large, even developing the character of civil war. This was the case in the Russian Revolution and in the Mexican Revolution that began in 1910.

The changes that are brought into being by a revolution should be something new in the history of that society. If instead they restore preexisting structures that had passed away, the event may be referred to as a counterrevolution, rather than a revolution. The economic changes brought about by a revolution are also normally expected to improve the conditions of life for the poorer members of society or those lower in the social hierarchy.

As the term is usually used, accordingly, a revolution is a change in the location of political power that begins a process of fundamental social and economic change, introducing practices novel in that society, which tend to benefit those lower in social status. Because this set of expectations attaches to the concept of revolution it is always possible for a revisionist historian to excite interest with a documentation of the case that a specific revolution deviated from expectations in one of these aspects. One example of this is the assertion that the American Revolution was really a counterrevolution in that it was fought to restore privileges that had been taken away from the colonists by George III; or, similarly, that the wars for the independence of the Latin American countries were really counterrevolutionary in that they were supported by members of the wealthier classes who feared that a new liberal government in Spain might legislate reforms advantageous to the poorer members of society.

II

The simplest attempts to explain the occurrence of revolutions rely on the extent of oppression suffered by the lower classes, or perhaps the middle classes, under the old regime: "The people were so oppressed that finally they could take it no longer." In point of fact, however, as many historians have pointed out in concrete cases, the simple fact of oppression does not lead to revolution. Lower classes stay oppressed for century after century without rising in revolt.

A classic work by the historian Crane Brinton, *The Anatomy of Revolution*, examined four major revolutions and found various circumstances common to all of them.[1] The political scientist James Davies synthesized a variety of previous works, including that of Brinton, in a now-classic article that identified the critical cause of revolution as the frustration of rising expectations.[2] This drew on the observations of various scholars that social and economic conditions, especially for the social class immediately below the ruling class of the old regime, had in fact improved for a substantial period of time prior to the onset of the revolution, but then conditions had suddenly deteriorated immediately before the revolution, or political constraints had prevented the improvement from continuing, or political constraints had prevented the economic and social gains won by the rising class from being translated into political power.

Another way of formulating this last insight is in terms of one of the major principles of Aristotle's political science, that the distribution of political power tends to approximate the distribution of wealth. If a new middle class is becoming more affluent, that is, it will want to acquire political power appropriate to its new status. If prevented from doing so by the political system as it exists, it will act to change that political system. Contemporary political scientists, in their own jargon, might say that the revolution was due to the enhanced sense of political efficacy that the new middle class had derived from its improved economic situation. Karl Marx might rephrase Aristotle's insight to say that the political superstructure must come to reflect the changed economic substructure. In any event, most observers would rest content with the notion that a new, more economically affluent middle class had seized the political power appropriate to its new situation; the old ruling class, which had lost control and the economic means of sustaining its position, was swept away; and the new rulers then proceeded to restructure society in line with their preferences and interests.

III

A counterrevolution, on the other hand, would then be the attempt to restore a preexisting social and economic order, or to prevent a new one from emerging, by a class whose position threatened to decline, but which still retained enough political power to prevent social evolution from taking the course it would otherwise have followed. A classic instance of a counterrevolution in these terms would be the overthrow of the Weimar Republic and seizure of political power by Adolf Hitler in Germany in 1933. While Hitler found support, at different times, from members of various social classes, the core of his following consisted of lower middle-class and upper working-class elements whose economic and social status was being threatened by economic changes in German society, but who retained enough political power to resist change through their votes. In this they were supported by key elements in German society left over from the Imperial era which had held onto power during the Weimar period, even though they were out of tune with the new republican order: the military, the higher bureaucracy and the judiciary, and the magnates of heavy industry. These elite elements were later added to the core of Hitler's electoral support, which consisted of small farmers whose well-being was threatened by the growth of agribusiness and by the control of farm prices by middlemen and brokers; artisans and handcraft workers whose market was threatened by the development of cheaper factory production; and small shopkeepers threatened with being put out of business by the development of department stores and chain stores. One of the interesting aspects of this story is that Hitler was quite well aware of which social groups should make up his electoral base

and why. This comes through clearly in his comments on one
of his political idols, the mayor of Vienna, Karl Lueger:

> Lueger based his party first of all on the middle class
> which was threatened with extinction, and thus secured
> a class of adherents extremely hard to shake, ready both
> [sic] for great sacrifices and capable of stubborn fighting.[3]

It should be noted that Hitler wanted adherents who would
not only vote for him but would if necessary fight in the streets
as well. And, foreshadowing his own later success in convincing
some of the leaders of heavy industry to provide him with funds,
Hitler said of Lueger that he "was prepared to make use of all
available means of power to attract to himself strong existing
institutions." Appealing, as he did, to groups of people whose
economic interests were objectively in conflict, such as the urban lower-middle class, farmers, and capitalists, Hitler faced
the problem of reconciling mutually contradictory appeals to
create an image of credibility and sincerity, rather than in-
consistency and opportunism. This he did through his use of
anti-Semitism, by creating an image, for working-class supporters, of the Jewish capitalist; for industrialist supporters,
of the Jewish labor agitator; for the farmer, of the Jewish land
speculator; and for the shopkeeper, of the Jewish department
storeowner.[4]

IV

More careful consideration of the problem of explaining the
occurrence of revolutions, however, suggests that in the fore-
going discussion we may have been making the problem too
complex and its resolution too esoteric. As was noted, a revolution in the full sense is a complex event involving a shift in
the holders of power, extensive violence, and fundamental social and economic change. Retrospective explanations, accordingly, deal with major dimensions of social and economic
causality. The causes of such a major event must have been
grand shifts in social class structure, major developments in
technology, or the reconstruction of attitudes and values. In

point of fact, however, in some cases the revolution may have become a "revolution" only in retrospect. That is, the causality of the revolution may be adequately explained if the causes of merely its initial phase are accounted for. This is so because sometimes the process itself is the cause of its own amplification into a major historical event.

The Cuban Revolution provides a good illustration of what is meant. The Cuban Revolution certainly qualifies as a "true" revolution, in that it changed the nature of the Cuban economy and Cuban social structure, led to the exodus of a substantial percentage of the national population, and caused a drastic reorientation of the country's foreign policy. Nevertheless, these results were not implicit in the first events, those for which causes need to be found, of the process. At the time, there certainly seemed no compelling historical reason that the Cuban Revolution could not have been simply the replacement of a dictatorship by an elected civilian government, with no further changes in economic and social structure or in foreign policy, such as is in fact a frequent occurrence in Latin America. There were certainly important forces in the movement that took power in Cuba on January 1, 1959, that would have confined the Revolution to such dimensions. The first president of the Revolution, Manuel Urrutia Lleó, and its first prime minister, José Miró Cardona, would certainly have been content if the Revolution had stopped at that point. So would the government of the United States, the major force in the politics of the region. It took an effort out of the normal, something that could not reliably have been predicted on the basis of what had gone before, to produce the final results of the Cuban Revolution. It seems difficult to deny that the ideas and personality of the leader of the Revolution, Fidel Castro, were crucial in determining which direction was taken, and that therefore separate explanations are needed to understand why Fidel Castro came to power and why he followed the policies he did. Grand historical explanations relying on long-term shifts in Cuban society and economy may well overexplain. One may need only to know why Batista was overthrown and why Fidel chose one set of policies rather than another.

The same kind of observation can be made of another of the

great revolutions of the twentieth century, the Mexican Revolution. That too led to major changes in society and the economy, in politics, social structure, and foreign policy. It resulted in the redistribution of land, the nationalization of railroads and the petroleum industry, and the subordination of the military to civilian authority. Explanations of the Mexican Revolution in terms of long-term economic shifts that were going on in the late nineteenth century have been advanced. Certainly such changes were going on, but they were going on as well in Argentina and Brazil and other countries that did not experience a revolution of the Mexican kind. The present writer would argue that what we regard now as the Mexican Revolution grew out of the process of civil war that was unleashed by the way the events of the first phase of the Revolution developed. That is, the goals of the initial leader of the Mexican Revolution, Francisco Madero, were limited to replacing the existing dictator, Porfirio Díaz, and eliminating corruption, which did not envisage the fundamental social and economic changes that eventually gave the Revolution its character. There seems no reason to believe that had Madero remained in power the Revolution could not have ended with achievements of this type, with the country then resuming the moderate path of historical evolution it had been following. However, with the assassination of Madero and the imposition of a new military dictatorship by Victoriano Huerta, fighting became more and more extensive until most of the country was caught up in a civil war. This war itself then became the major factor ensuring that social change would be far-reaching. Hitherto apathetic peasants were socially mobilized as they became involved in the fighting. The extent of the sacrifices made in the war could only be justified if its outcome was substantial change; and, finally, extensive social reform became the condition for the restoration of stability. Only the institution of such reforms would lead armed workers and peasants to support a stable government. This was clearly demonstrated when victory in the fighting that attended the revolt led by Adolfo de la Huerta in 1923 was won by Alvaro Obregón and Plutarco Elías Calles. They were able to attract more mass support than de la Huerta because their government had been responsible for land reform and legislation protecting workers' rights. The process of fighting, that is, had a logic of its own and shaped the nature of the Revolution.

This point has been appreciated by Régis Debray in his attempt to draw lessons from the Cuban Revolution that could be applied to the fomenting of revolution elsewhere in Latin America.[5] In contravention of classic Marxist doctrine that a revolution occurs when social and economic conditions have become ripe for it, Debray argued that the Cuban Revolution had shown that the conditions for revolution could be created by the process of revolution itself; that if a nucleus of dedicated revolutionaries began a guerrilla war, then the process of repression by the government, the consequent alienation of the population, and the organization of the peasants by the guerrilla nucleus could escalate until a successful revolution took place. While in fact no Latin American revolutions using the Debray formula have succeeded, this may be due less to the inadequacy of his theoretical insight than to the fact that governments (including that of the United States), alerted to the problem by the success of the Cuban Revolution—and by the writings of Debray and others—have made a point of putting down would-be guerrilla nuclei before they become firmly established.

V

Whether a complete social revolution was envisaged at the time of the seizure of power, or whether the hopes for a final end to the people's misery only developed as fighting progressed, the victorious revolutionary regime is faced with hopes and expectations that are, given the obduracy of the economic and psychological problems that face any attempts to ameliorate the human condition, regrettably unrealistic. The successful revolution faces very real external enemies, in the vanquished social classes that may attempt to regroup and resume power, and in foreign opponents of the revolution who may seek to combat it by arms or by economic pressure and boycott. But even if such external enemies be defeated or held at bay, every revolution faces at least partial defeat at the

hands of its major internal enemy: the refusal of human behavior to adapt to the requirements of the new dispensation.

The difficulty here is that not all of the evils of the old regime
are due to its perverted institutions and its corrupt leadership.
Some of them are due to inevitable accompaniments of the
human condition, the selfishness bred into all of us by evolution, without which we and our families would starve, and the
inequality of status inherent in any organization of social and
economic tasks more complicated than the foraging and farming of the most primitive gathering or agricultural societies.
If the revolutionary government makes one of its primary objectives the reformation of behavior in a puritanical sense, as
in the French Revolution, the reaction will be swift. Human
beings seem capable of totally altruistic and self-denying behavior only for short periods. If new norms of public-spiritedness, collective effort, and equality of reward are built into the
economic arrangements established by the revolution, the reaction may not be sudden and political, but may take the form
of sabotage of the new arrangements, low productivity, and the
growth of an illegal economy alongside the legal one.

There are many things wrong with an economy based on
economic incentives and inequality of reward, and the social
character it produces is not as admirable as that of the altruistic
patriot. But the attempt to base a society on equality and public
spirit meets with so little success that all too often governments
supplement purely moral incentives with physical disincen-
tives in the form of punitive laws and petty spying, with the
paradoxical result that revolutionary regimes that attempt to
inculcate moral principles of public-spiritedness and altruism
find themselves relying instead on spying, coercion, and punishment. It should be pointed out that some revolutionary regimes are much worse offenders than others in this regard, and
not all of them end in the terror and arbitrary executions of
the Stalinist era in the Soviet Union or the Cultural Revolution
in Communist China. It is certainly true nevertheless that
experience with the excesses of revolutionary regimes serves
to convince their populations of the value of civil liberties.

In order to proceed the faster with its reconstruction of society, the revolutionary regime also dispenses with the checks

and balances of liberal constitutional systems, the opposition in the legislature, the independent courts, and the like, only to find that an absence of opposition also means an absence of constructive criticism. As a result, costly major errors are made. Experience with revolutionary regimes, in other words, serves to demonstrate the merits of the traditional constitutional patterns that have evolved in the West, with all their faults, that allow for a measure of economic freedom, guarantees of civil liberties, and the freedom to criticize government policy and propose alternatives.

NOTES

1. Crane Brinton, *The Anatomy of Revolution*, Englewood Cliffs, NJ: Prentice Hall, 1952.
2. James Davies, "Toward a Theory of Revolution," *American Sociological Review*, February 1962.
3. Adolf Hitler, *Mein Kampf* (in the translation published as *My Battle*), Boston: Houghton Mifflin, 1935, p. 43.
4. See Martin C. Needler, "Hitler's Anti-Semitism: A Political Appraisal," *Public Opinion Quarterly* 24(4), Winter 1960.
5. Régis Debray, *Revolution in the Revolution?* (translated by Bobbye Ortiz), New York: Grove Press, 1967.

2

TOTALITARIANISM AND DICTATORSHIP

I

The term "totalitarianism" came into vogue among political scientists in the late 1940s and early 1950s. It was based on the premise that the Stalinist government of the Soviet Union shared enough features with the Nazi tyranny in Germany that the two could be considered as belonging to the same political type. This view represented something of an innovation, since under the previously prevailing system of categories, they had been regarded as polar opposites—the one a government of the extreme left, the other of the extreme right. The insight that a single structure and dynamics could be found beneath the differences in rhetoric and explicit ideology had its most convincing formulation in George Orwell's novel *1984*.

And yet the "totalitarianism" formulation creates problems as much as it solves them. When two items—of any kind—are placed in the same category, what happens is that the characteristics they have in common are stressed but the differences between them are minimized. This procedure may be misleading if those differences are in fact significant. Moreover, since a set containing only two members seems rather empty, the attempt was naturally made to fill up the "totalitarian" category with further examples, and some regimes were included only at the cost of grossly distorting their actual character. The most serious problem, however, and one that always arises when actually existent entities are placed in categories defined *a priori*, is that characteristics of the abstract model are imputed to the entity in the real world, yet the real-world entity never displays the full range of traits defined as characterizing the abstract model. The temptation is very strong to insist that they are there nevertheless, so that a device designed to facilitate understanding may come eventually to obstruct it.

Specifically, in the most widely cited definition of the totalitarian system, that of Carl J. Friedrich and Zbigniew Brzezinski, a totalitarian system is said to have an official ideology, a single authorized political party typically led by one man, a political police that uses terror, a monopoly on communications and on weapons, and a centrally directed economy.[1] Even so limited and self-evident a set of defining characteristics as these, however, indicates strongly that the model is preeminently a generalization from the characteristics of the Soviet Union under Stalin. Many regimes commonly referred to as totalitarian do not measure up to these defining characteristics of the model. Mussolini's regime, for example, which originated the word "fascist," seems not to have been totalitarian by this definition. The autonomy left to the Catholic Church, which had its own communications network, certainly denied the regime a communications monopoly. The extent to which Mussolini had a distinctive ideology may also be questioned. As the dictator's own article for the *Enciclopedia Italiana* indicated, what passed for ideology was mostly verbiage rationalizing an unscrupulous opportunism. Questions can even be raised, and indeed have been raised by careful historians working in the aftermath of World War II, about whether Hitler's Germany was totalitarian in the full sense. The economy remained in private hands, and was largely controlled by private decision-makers. Factories did not even go on three shifts until late in the war. We know now that Hitler never had complete control of his army, in which the traditional Prussian conservative ethos remained strong; witness the several military plots against him. Neither did he have complete control of his counterintelligence service, the *Abwehr*, whose director, Admiral Canaris, was negotiating and, to some extent, even collaborating with the Allies during the war. This point is extremely important, because enthusiasm for their model leads Friedrich and Brzezinski to say that successful revolution is not possible in a totalitarian regime. This assertion, however, is true only insofar as it is tautological. That is, if the totalitarian dictator does indeed have total control of everything and everybody in the society, then of course revolution is not possible by definition; but in fact in societies that we call totalitarian it is possible for this total control to be lost or even never to have been achieved in the first place.

One can clearly see the errors of interpretation and policy that can arise from the assumption that a regime necessarily embodies all of the traits defined as characteristic of the category into which it has been put: Do not waste resources supporting the resistance against Hitler, since that cause is by definition hopeless; there is no point in framing disarmament proposals so as to strengthen the hand of a hypothetical anti-military faction in the Politburo, since the leadership is necessarily monolithic; the Sandinistas may promise to permit opposition parties and a substantial private economic sector, but we know *a priori* that such things could not be possible under their rule. At the time of writing, the "essentialist" attitude, the view that the Soviet regime, for example, embodies the characteristics ascribed to the totalitarian model as a necessary and unchangeable part of its nature, takes the form of the belief that the changes introduced by Secretary Gorbachev are inevitably doomed to failure or are perhaps only an elaborate public relations charade to deceive the West. This attitude, which says "I already know the truth of everything; I am not interested in new evidence," is of course quite unscientific. It is the nature of scientific knowledge to be continuously revised as new data become available.

II

This point leads us to a more sophisticated approach to the problem of totalitarianism, which is to say that totalitarianism—the total control of the thoughts and behavior of everyone in the society—should be regarded not as a reality but as an aspiration to which some (but not all) dictators strive. A dictatorship may thus be more or less totalitarian; it can never be perfectly totalitarian, since in the nature of things the absolute control aspired to by the dictator is physically not possible to achieve. This perspective then draws our attention to the fact that totalitarianism is not an accomplished situation, but a dynamic process, which consists of the attempt to establish control successively over all of the institutions of the society. This approach restores a distinction between left-wing and right-wing totalitarianism, or at least between postrevolutionary leftist regimes that create their own institutions after destroying those of the *ancien régime*, and the right-wing totalitarian regimes that primarily attempt to take over (*gleichschalten*, or to coordinate or syncromesh) institutions that were already in existence.

When the totalitarian movement attempts to assert its control over existing institutions, totalitarianism can most fruitfully be understood not as a set of related characteristics that form an ideal type, but rather as a process of the increasing actualization of totalitarian goals. This focus on the problem also enables us to understand the behavior of the totalitarian movement once it has achieved power, and also to understand the reasons for its ultimate failure.

An instructive example is provided by the case of Juan Perón in Argentina. Although he first emerged as a major political figure in the context of an authoritarian military regime that had seized power, Perón subsequently was elected president in his own right. He then proceeded to impose his authority successively over each of the major institutions of Argentina's plural society. As secretary of labor he had already established control of the unions, replacing their leadership with people personally loyal to him. His majority in the legislature enabled him to remove members of the Supreme Court legally, by impeachment, and replace them with his own appointees. Unsympathetic university professors were removed and replaced, and compulsory courses in "Peronism" were introduced. Peronist officers were favored in armed forces promotions, courses in the principles of Peronism appeared in military schools, and officers were required to take an oath of loyalty to Perón personally, not simply to the Argentine state. Opposition newspapers were intimidated and closed.

As Perón moved to extend his control throughout society, however, victories became successively more difficult to achieve. His control of the army was never complete, and of the navy only minimal. The totalitarian drive finally foundered on the rock of Peter; like other dictators in Catholic countries, Perón found that although the Church's cooperation might be obtained for a time, it could never be brought completely under control.

Initially, Perón had conciliated the Church, reintroducing compulsory religious education in the schools. Apparently becoming concerned that the lay movement Catholic Action could provide a focus of political opposition, Perón later reversed himself and tried to weaken the Church by taking an anticlerical line, legislating to permit divorce and prostitution, and even attempting to reduce attendance at mass by having worshippers arrested as they entered or left church. His excommunication provided the catalyst for the conspiracy that finally overthrew him.

Similarly, Communist Poland provided a case in which a government totalitarian in principle had to limit the extent of its control in order to make space for the indigestible Polish Catholic Church. The point here is that the observer should not simply place a government in the "totalitarian" category and then assume that it necessarily displays all of the traits of the totalitarian ideal type. This was the fallacy committed by the erstwhile political scientist Jeane Kirkpatrick in the famous article that, according to reports, first drew her to Ronald Reagan's attention and led to her appointment as U.S. ambassador to the United Nations.[2] Using the conventional political science distinction between totalitarian governments and non-totalitarian dictatorships or authoritarian regimes, which do not aspire to control the whole of society and are therefore in some sense "not as bad" as totalitarian regimes, Dr. Kirkpatrick in effect placed all left-wing governments in the totalitarian and all right-wing governments in the merely

authoritarian category, thus providing the intellectual justification for a U.S. policy of opposing left-wing but not right-
wing dictatorships.

Of course, only in the pages of *1984* does a perfect totalitarian
state exist. In the real world governments fall far short of the
ideal type. Even a government that identifies itself as Communist, such as those of Poland or Cuba, may in fact be less
repressive to its subjects than a right-wing authoritarian government of a more traditional type. Thus in Latin America, for
example, the Cuban government under Fidel Castro, although
repressive, is clearly less repressive than was the personalist
dictatorship of Rafael Trujillo in the Dominican Republic
(1930–61). In point of fact, the most totalitarian government
seen in the western hemisphere was probably that of Trujillo.
This was a non-ideological personalist regime in which the
newspapers devoted themselves to praising the "Benefactor's"
exploits; the capital city, which Trujillo renamed after himself,
was filled with his likenesses, and people were afraid to talk
because the dictator's spies were everywhere. Since Trujillo
was involved in all aspects of the economy, amassing himself
a colossal fortune, and since his son and namesake was placed
in command of the major military base dominating the capital,
the Trujillo regime seems to have exhibited all of the characteristics of the Friedrich-Brzezinski model of totalitarianism
except that it lacked an ideology. The cult of the dictator
seemed to perform the functions discharged by the official ideology elsewhere.

Examples such as that of Trujillo make clear that it is misleading to regard traditional dictatorships and totalitarian systems as different types. The case is simply that some
dictatorships are more totalitarian than others; it is a question
of degree rather than of kind. It is equally mistaken to regard
totalitarianism as peculiarly a creation of the twentieth century, made possible only by the technological changes in communications of recent years. Twentieth-century totalitarian
systems actually resemble in many respects the fanatical religious dictatorships of earlier times, like that of Calvin in
Geneva, in which the insistence on religious orthodoxy went

hand in hand with a secret police, repression of opposition, and so on.

The further argument that leftist "totalitarian" regimes differ from and are more to be resisted than merely authoritarian rightist regimes because the rule of the former is irreversible represents a misperception of the facts.[3] The "totalitarian" Communist regimes of Eastern Europe remained in power not because of any essential characteristic of their nature, but only because the Red Army stood ready to intervene to maintain them in power. In fact, without such intervention the history of Hungary, East Germany, Poland, and Czechoslovakia has already demonstrated that "totalitarian" rule is reversible—or that "totalitarianism" is only a conceptual ideal type. Existent regimes can never be fully totalitarian.

III

It is equally true that we have been misled in the construction of the concept of totalitarianism by the perception of similarities between the Hitler and Stalin systems. Similarities certainly exist, but the emphasis on similarities should not be allowed to obscure the very important differences between the two systems. Hitler rose to power in a democratic system and continued to use many of the techniques of the candidate for office. He made powerful speeches that were designed to convince and to move. Attempts to overthrow his regime from the preexisting conservative institutions that he let stand, the bureaucracy and the military, were inhibited by awareness of his very considerable popular support, and by the technical legality of his accession to power. At the same time, Hitler's motivating ambition was always to refight World War I, to exact revenge from France, and to conquer territory in the East at the expense of Poland and Russia.

Stalin was quite different in these respects. His route to power led not through elections and rallies but through bureaucratic manipulation, built on committees, shifts of personnel, alignments, and coalitions. The Bolsheviks, despite their name, knew they were a minority that had seized power and

were beset by internal enemies attempting, with support from
Western intelligence agencies, to overthrow them. Stalin's totalitarianism, unlike Hitler's, was aimed not at expansion but
at holding on to what he had. The policy issue on which he
defeated Trotsky was precisely that of trying to defend existing
positions rather than make new advances abroad, and in this
he was supported by the new state and party bureaucracy,
concerned with safety and stability. Identification of the Stalin
and Hitler systems can thus lead the observer to misinterpret
Stalin's expansionism, which was cautious and pragmatic, by
confounding it with the reckless bellicosity of the Nazis.

Some similarities between the two regimes derived from the
totalitarian impulse, although in the case of Hitler this was
apparently based more on pure ambition, while in the case of
Stalin it seems to have been based primarily on fears, initially
justified although later becoming paranoid, of real opposition
to and conspiracies against his rule. Some of the minor similarities of style and organization, moreover, developed not out
of necessity but out of imitation. On Hitler's part, some of these
were conscious imitations of Mussolini, a former socialist, who
had copied Lenin.

Totalitarianism is thus best understood as an extreme form
of dictatorship, in which the dictator aspires to total control.
It is to mistake accidental characteristics for essential ones to
regard it, as Friedrich and Brzezinski do, as "a logical extension
of certain traits of our modern industrial society." Totalitarianism today will of course use the currently available techniques. These may be the two-way telescreens of *1984* or the
ability to recognize individual voice prints on a tapped tele-
phone of Solzhenitsyn's novel, *First Circle*. They may be the
techniques of 1984 or 1933 or 1640. The essential structural
features of the system, however, are not contingent on a given
level of technology.

IV

Dictatorship is normally regarded as the antithesis of democracy, but as Franz Neumann has reminded us, there are
also cases of dictatorships that prepare for democracy and dic-

tatorships that save democracy.[4] We have an example of the dictatorship that prepares for democracy in the last phase of the rule of an imperial power that has decided to relinquish its authority to representatives of the indigenous population. Following World War II, in most territories of the British Empire, colonial authorities made a systematic attempt to organize a gradual transition from bureaucratic imperial rule to elected indigenous rule through a series of stages that would habituate elected local officials to functioning within a Westminster type of parliamentary system. Each new system would then continue to operate after the Union Jack had been lowered and the British governor recalled to London. In the West Indies, India, and the South Pacific, that hope has largely been realized. In Africa, however, the parliamentary systems left behind were generally transformed into authoritarian regimes not long after the British left. Preparation for democracy clearly has to entail a long process of education and acculturation if it is to be effective, and it must be able as well to count on favorable economic and social circumstances. During such a drawn-out period of training, a "tutelary dictatorship" may exist that legitimizes itself in terms of its educational function. Even the great libertarian John Stuart Mill wrote that an authoritarian government was justified in such circumstances.[5] The difficulty here is that all kinds of authoritarian governments attempt to legitimize themselves by citing the people's lack of sufficient education and sophistication to operate a democratic regime. Claims to be operating a tutelary regime may be quite false, however, if no attempt whatsoever is made to prepare the way for democracy.

The most common case of the tutelary regime today is the single-party system. The single-party system is worthy of an extended discussion of its own, which will be conducted in Chapter 6.

The dictatorship to save democracy, at first sight a paradoxical concept, is not as strange as it appears. The original Roman institution of dictatorship was in fact a temporary emergency measure strictly limited in time. Of course, the problem with a temporary dictatorship to defend republican institutions is that it is subject to abuse and may instead be used to subvert republican institutions and perpetuate single-man authoritarian rule. To avoid this contingency, the Romans provided a drastic remedy: The dictatorship was limited to a period of six months, and if a dictator did not withdraw from the office at the conclusion of that time, he could legally be killed by anyone.

Today, many countries follow the Roman law tradition by provision for a "state of siege," under which executive authorities are freed from procedural restraints in the arrest and detention of suspects. The principal safeguard against abuse is that a state of siege is generally limited in time. This limitation may, however, be circumvented. In Paraguay, the declaration of a state of siege automatically lapses after 90 days. However, the government of General Stroessner, which has at the time of writing just been overthrown after 35 years in power, throughout that time, with only brief exceptions, simply issued a new declaration of a state of siege each time the existing one lapsed.

A related mode of attempting to limit the development of an authoritarian regime by putting a time limit on it has been adopted throughout Latin America in the form of the prohibition against presidential reelection, written in some form into the constitution of almost every country in Latin America. A president may thus abuse his power, but the period of such abuse is limited by the end of a single legal term of office. (In some countries he may return to office after skipping one or two terms.) The prohibition of reelection constitutes a clear marker, a Rubicon that a would-be dictator has to pass, thereby signalling his intentions and, perhaps, providing the last straw for the organization of a conspiracy to overthrow him.

This is a critical element in organizing resistance to a tyranny: being able to establish clearly where the dictator has passed the bounds of legitimate behavior. The fact, for example, that Hitler always maintained a color of legality for his regime served to neutralize much would-be opposition, especially in the bureaucracy and the army. This is one reason that it is so regrettable that the constitution of the French Fifth Republic, for example, in its provisions for a state of emergency in Article 16, does not effectively restrict the president's power to declare an emergency and to take any measures he sees fit on his own authority. There is no clear point at which a French president who wishes to make himself a dictator signals such an intention by passing the legal boundaries of his powers. In this respect, as in others, the constitution of the Fifth Republic resembles that of the Weimar Republic.

NOTES

1. Carl J. Friedrich and Zbigniew Brzezinski, *Totalitarian Government and Autocracy*, Cambridge, Mass.: Harvard University Press, 1956.

2. Jeane Kirkpatrick, "Dictatorships and Double Standards," *Commentary*, November 1979, pp. 34–35.

3. Wayne King, "Presidential Politics" (interview with Jeane Kirkpatrick), *New York Times*, November 2, 1987, page 14.

4. Franz Neumann, *The Democratic and Authoritarian State*, Glencoe, Ill: Free Press, 1957, p. 248.

5. "What they" [a people used to slavery] "require is not a government of force, but one of guidance," but "I need scarcely remark that leading-strings are only admissible as a means of gradually training the people to walk alone." John Stuart Mill, *Utilitarianism, Liberty, and Representative Government*, 1910, Everyman's Library, London: J. M. Dent & Sons; New York: E. P. Dutton, 1947, p. 199.

3

LEGITIMACY

People obey constituted authorities in part out of habit and in part because of fear of the consequences of disobedience. For a regime to be most secure in its subjects' loyalty, however, the subjects need also to believe that the regime's authority is legitimate; not that it is simply there, or that it has the ability to punish disobedience, but that it has for some reason a right to command their obedience. Whether or not a government is perceived as legitimate is significant in commanding the obedience not only of the citizens at large, but more especially of its instruments of rule: the bureaucracy, the police, and the armed forces. When habits of obedience are weak and the government's ability to enforce compliance is in question, belief in its legitimacy can still be a powerful inhibitor to organization of and support for conspiracies to overthrow it.[1]

I

What are the bases of a regime's legitimacy? Why do citizens believe that specific governments have the right to command their obedience? The classic treatment of this problem is given by Max Weber, who distinguished three types of legitimate authority: traditional, charismatic, and rational-legal. These categories have continued to dominate thinking about legitimacy. Charismatic authority was that enjoyed by a ruler believed to have attributes—of mind, spirit, or perhaps physical ability—that placed him above the normal run of humankind, giving him the right to command obedience. Rational-legal authority was typically authority exercised by honest administrators chosen on merit, derived from a written constitution and a body of laws that seemed reasonably designed to achieve generally accepted purposes. Traditional authority was authority validated by being acquired in a manner sanctified by time, typically inheritance of a crown in a monarchic system.

Before beginning his discussion of legitimate authority Weber made clear that obedience was often based on material interests, ties of affection, or ideological solidarity. Legitimacy itself derived from none of these things, however, but solely from belief in the regime's right to rule.[2] Weber subsumes both democratic and revolutionary legitimacy into the charismatic type, and seems by rational-legal authority to be thinking especially of a *Rechtsstaat* of the Prussian type, that is, a system based on the rule of law and run by an honest and efficient bureaucracy, but which is not necessarily democratic.

In Weber's lexicon, these are "ideal types." That is, any actual case may involve some mixture of the three types of authority in different degrees; perhaps every case does so. Thus a king's authority may be regarded as legitimate not only because he is the rightful heir to the throne and thus has traditional legitimacy, but also because he has signified his willingness to govern by generally accepted laws adopted by a parliament—rational-legal authority. The trappings of monarchy always in any case impart an aura of charisma: "There's a divinity doth hedge a king." But the difficulty with Weber's categories goes beyond that of the ideal type which is never perfectly reflected in a concrete case. The test of a typology is its usefulness, whether it clarifies issues and enables us to see things that might otherwise have been obscure. What it should not do is cause us to blur significant distinctions or misunderstand what is really happening. This problem becomes especially signifi-

cant in determining the extent to which a regime has lost
legitimacy, which investigation has shown is critical in determining if people are willing to join in an attempt to overthrow
it. In fact, it is precisely when the continued existence of a
government is in doubt that questions of legitimacy become
acute.

II

A recent example of the attempted overthrow of a government can provide an illuminating starting point for analysis.
On February 23, 1981, an attempt to overthrow the government
of Spain posed the question of legitimacy in particularly striking form. The attempted seizure of power involved the occupation of the parliament building as the Cortes was preparing
to vote to confirm a new cabinet in office. At the same time,
the attempt was made to recruit key military commanders to
the side of the insurgents, in part by conveying to them the
impression that the coup had the backing of the king. (Since
the death of the dictator Francisco Franco in 1975, Spain has
been a monarchy.) The king's support was to be secured, in
case he should prove reluctant, by convincing him that a united
military was behind the coup and that any opposition to it
would occasion bloodshed. The success of the coup thus required
a double bluff: The military commanders had to be convinced
that the king was behind the coup while the king had to be
convinced that the military commanders were behind it. Meanwhile, parliament was to be coerced into conferring legitimacy
on the leadership that would emerge from the coup by voting
it legally into office.

In fact, the conspirators finally capitulated after a night in
which the king made it clear to them, to military commanders
he contacted by phone, and to the public, which he addressed
on television, that in fact he opposed the attempted seizure of
power. Following the defeat of the coup, the leaders of all the
political parties called at the palace to present their compli-
ments to the king. Subsequently, all of the parties' leaders,
from ultra-conservative to Communist, led a demonstration in
which the crowd shouted "*Vivas!*" to democracy and to the king.

Clearly, this was a sequence of events in which the position of King Juan Carlos was critical. How was this possible, when the monarchy had only been restored for a few years, when the monarch had been picked (in the sense that there were at least three possible contenders) by Franco, a dictator whose rule was resented by at least half the population, and had then been tutored under Franco's supervision? The government that Franco had overthrown had been in any case a republic rather than a monarchy, and Spain had not been a monarchy for over 50 years.

The legitimacy question was especially acute for officers of the armed forces. Officers had been formed during the years of the Franco regime to regard socialism, liberalism, and even democracy as subversive doctrines of foreign origin. Yet after the death of Franco the Caudillo's successors had presided over the drafting, and approval in a popular referendum, of a standard Western democratic constitution, with its apparatus of elections, political parties, and guarantees of individual rights. The Communist Party was legalized and statutes of autonomy were granted to the Basque country and Catalonia, authorizing practices that would, under Franco, have been regarded as treasonable subversion of the unity of the Spanish state. Yet presiding over these developments, and selecting the prime minister who put them through, was Juan Carlos de Borbón, trained in the military academies of the dictatorship, and picked as his successor by Franco, who had told the military, "Obey the king as you would me."

Against the conspirators, therefore, Juan Carlos could call on the following sources of legitimacy:

1. According to military regulations, the king was commander-in-chief, with ultimate command responsibility. Within the military, he thus had rational-legal legitimacy.

2. For committed falangist authoritarians, Juan Carlos was the chosen successor of Franco, who had ordered them to obey him. In Weberian terms, there were both traditional and charismatic elements in this source of author-

ity. The king had inherited his authority from Franco, who had ruled in the name of traditional values; yet Franco was "the Caudillo," who ruled on the basis of his superior personal claims, and some of his charisma was transferred in his anointment of the young king.

3. A segment of the officer corps was ideologically monarchist. In fact, the officer corps may be the only segment of society in which genuine monarchist sentiments survive. For officers of this type, the Franco dictatorship was always only the second-best alternative. Although this kind of monarchism represented a reservoir of support for Juan Carlos, it should be noted that both principal leaders of the attempted seizure of power in February were confirmed monarchists. However, the monarchy they supported would have been more absolutist than the English-style constitutional monarchy which Juan Carlos wisely believed was likely to prove most stable in the circumstances of the late twentieth century. In this sense, it was possible to be more monarchist than the king.

4. A relatively small segment within the Spanish armed forces of the time, although the largest among civilians, consisted of those committed to a democratic Spain and a politically neutral armed forces. People adhering to this view had generally not supported Juan Carlos previously but only gave him support because of the position he took opposing the coup; they subsequently became supporters of the limited monarchy he represented, although most of them had previously been republican in sentiment. The democratic view drew from Spain's own democratic tradition, but was also influenced by the political culture of the Europe that Spain aspired to join, as well as by the more general "Atlantic" culture that dominates the media of communications in the West today. While democratic officers were relatively few within the armed forces, they had been placed in key positions in military intelligence by the king and the defense minister so that they could monitor conspiracies in process of formation.

Bearing in mind this set of circumstances, we are now in a position to reexamine the question of legitimacy critically. Monarchy is clearly a traditional form of authority, in which the right to rule is inherited, except in the case of charismatic claims by the founder of a new dynasty. Let us, however, focus on the support of King Juan Carlos by those of democratic persuasion. They accepted his authority as legitimate not because he himself was chosen democratically, and not just because the constitution that created a monarchic head of state was adopted by a democratic referendum; he was supported because his continuance as monarch would make a democratic system possible. That is, for this kind of opinion his legitimacy lay not in his origins or title to office; it was not retrospective. It was rather prospective, in what his remaining in office made feasible.

For many democrats, moreover, what gave constitutional democracy its legitimacy was not its rational-legal character, or the charismatic attributes of people who might be elected by popular vote, as would be suggested by the Weberian model. Rather it was the system generally accepted in the countries of greatest prestige, those with which they wanted Spain to be identified. At the same time, there were democrats in Spain, as there are elsewhere, who regarded constitutional democracy as the most legitimate form of government because it offers the hope of being the least violent system. That is, systems that oppress and exclude must resort frequently to force, and they are likely also to be brought to an end by exercises of force. As the most tolerant of political systems, as "that form of government which divides us least," democracy may thus derive its legitimacy from the priority given to the value of civil peace.

In other words, the legitimacy of a political system may not be intrinsic to it, but may derive from its association, or compatibility, with other circumstances or conditions. This is true not only of democrats. For many Spanish monarchists the legitimacy of the monarchy derived from its traditional claims, to be sure; but more important for many, if not most, monarchists was that monarchy was identified with a certain set

of values and political preferences, and it was these and not
its origins that gave monarchy its legitimacy.

III

To summarize: Weber's distinction between reasons of ideological solidarity for supporting a government and belief in
its legitimacy, while technically correct, is misleading. In fact,
in many cases it appears that apparently sincere belief in a
regime's legitimacy is a secondary characteristic growing out
of considerations of political ideology and material interest.

Logically, it might be thought that people's views as to the
legitimacy of a regime were more fundamental to them than
their views on questions of policy, policy questions seeming
more ephemeral than questions of choice of regime. In practice,
however, the relationship seems rather to be reversed, with a
regime's legitimacy depending on the acceptability of policy
outcomes that it produces. Thus one's material or ideological
reasons for being favorably disposed to a government are not
separate from the question of its legitimacy, but affect perceptions of that legitimacy. Weber appears to allow this relationship in the case of charismatic regimes, for which policy failure
implies a loss of charisma, but the relationship seems also to
hold with respect to regimes whose claim to rule is based on
traditional or rational-legal grounds.

Of course, the merit of a typology, or system of categories,
is in the extent to which it is helpful in clarifying the subject
and making it understandable. For understanding the legitimacy of the regimes that exist today, however, Weber's typology emphasizes some distinctions that seem less important and
groups together cases that might better be understood separately. Thus, Weber's "charismatic" category would include
equally a U.S. President elected partly because of the attrac-
tiveness of his personality; an African leader, president for life
because of his role in securing the country's independence; or
an Iranian Ayatollah who claimed to be speaking directly for
God.[3] Let me suggest that we can more profitably regard these
cases as distinct, in fact as exemplifying the three dominant

types of legitimacy claims at the present time: democratic, revolutionary, and religious legitimacy, respectively.

IV

Democratic legitimacy is enjoyed by systems that rest ultimately on popular election. This seems the most plausible basis of legitimacy today, and even regimes that are not genuinely democratic attempt to maintain a façade of democratic legitimacy by organizing fraudulent elections. Religious legitimacy today can be found principally in Muslim states, although it is not so long ago that religious authority was claimed for the monarchies of Europe; British coins still claim, in abbreviated Latin, that Elizabeth is Queen "by the grace of God."

Revolutionary legitimacy has overtones of the other two types. The real core of the claim of revolutionary regimes to legitimacy is their success; if the revolution had not succeeded, they would not be in power. Success is a sort of mandate from history. But indirectly it is also the mandate of heaven: "We would not have won if God had not been on our side." With about the same degree of plausibility, a revolutionary regime also claims democratic legitimacy: "We won because the people were on our side." This argument is reminiscent of the position taken by the U.S. State Department during the 1920s, when it was trying to beat a retreat from Woodrow Wilson's policy of recognizing democratically chosen governments to the traditional policy of recognizing governments that had *de facto* control of a country. When the Department wanted to recognize some government that had come to power irregularly during this period, that is, not by elections, it would say something like: "Popular support of the government is indicated by the lack of effective opposition to its rule."[4]

But most of all, the revolution justifies itself by reference to a transcendent principle: national independence, popular welfare, freedom from oppression, honesty, social justice. Sometimes revolution is taken to mean all good things and subsequent regimes may vary their emphasis on the values it represents, depending on the needs of the moment. Although the Communist governments of Eastern Europe held a form of election, their claim to rule was based more fundamentally on revolutionary legitimacy, the revolution representing a mandate of history in a special sense, since proletarian revolution is a significant phase in the evolution of history in its Marxist version.

Analytically, the legitimacy of a system of government is distinct from the legitimacy of the title of any individual to rule in that system. Monarchy may be accepted as a system of government, but the current king may still be regarded as a usurper. This is true of legitimacy deriving from origins. With legitimacy deriving from performance, however, the case is rather different: A usurper of office may come to be accepted as legitimate because of the manner in which he rules and the beneficial results of his policies, but the system cannot acquire a legitimacy of performance independent of the acts of the incumbent. Similarly, a system may lose legitimacy because of the policy failures of the office holders that it produces. If legitimacy cumulates, it also erodes.

We know that, logically, values cannot be derived from facts, and grammatically an imperative cannot be deduced solely from a sentence in the indicative mood. Empirically, however, facts can create rights. A practice that goes without challenge for a period of time creates a presumptive right; "possession is nine points of the law." A ruffian who imposes himself by force of arms on a district from whose inhabitants he extorts tribute, guarding his turf against other similar ruffians, becomes, with the passage of a generation or two, a feudal lord legitimately owed tax, rent, and labor obligations in return for affording protection against invasion.[5]

Legitimacy grows as the years pass without policy disasters, lost wars, breakdowns in internal order, or economic failure. Events of this kind, however, especially if continued or repeated, can erode legitimacy.

V

Legitimacy is the capacity to command acceptance and obedience; as legitimacy declines, therefore, a government is more likely to be removed. In Latin America, the evidence shows, governments are more likely to be overthrown if they lack democratic legitimacy—if they were not democratically elected, or were elected only by narrow margins. They are also more likely to be overthrown if they preside over unsuccessful wars or periods of economic deterioration.[6]

To possess legitimacy, it should be noted, means not only that a government commands general obedience in society. Legitimacy means more specifically that it commands obedience of the bureaucracy and the military forces, which are critical in enabling it to rule. Legitimacy thus provides an answer to the cynic's riddle: If the citizen obeys the government because the government has a monopoly of force, why do the professional holders of military force obey the political leadership?

If a regime lacks legitimacy, it is more likely to be overthrown. Times of ideological transition, when older ideas of legitimacy no longer command support, are especially likely to be periods of turmoil in political life. Some of the newly independent countries of Africa have been able to create a new basis for government legitimacy in the struggle for independence, so long as the leader of that struggle survives and his party remains united. If the leader dies and/or the party splits, the government may lose its legitimacy, in which case no inhibitions remain to a military seizure of power and rule on the basis of force. A similar result occurred frequently in the newly independent states of Latin America, where the ending of colonial rule removed the monarchical "God's grace" basis for government legitimacy. In societies built on the exploitation of Indian serfs and African slaves, the alternative available basis of legitimacy, democratic legitimacy, was hardly plausible and governments lacked those inhibitions to revolt and military seizure of power that legitimacy can provide, with results that are all too well known.

NOTES

1. John S. Fitch III, *The Military Coup d'Etat as a Political Process*, Baltimore: Johns Hopkins University Press, 1977.

2. Max Weber, *Economy and Society*, Guenther Roth and Klaus

Wittich, eds., New York: Bedminster Press, 1968, vol. 1, pp. 212–13. The discussion of legitimacy continues to p. 288.

3. Ibid., pp. 266–69.

4. See Chapter 6, "Recognition of de facto Governments," in Martin C. Needler, *The United States and the Latin American Revolution*, Boston: Allyn & Bacon, 1972 (2nd ed., UCLA Latin American Center, 1977).

5. "No one who knows anything about early economic history can doubt that rent was originally, and for centuries, a tax imposed by the strong on the weak in consideration of a real or pretended protection of the tenant." J.E.T. Rogers, *The Economic Interpretation of History*, 3rd ed., 1894. Cited in Wilhelm Abel, *Agricultural Fluctuations in Europe from Thirteenth to the Twentieth Centuries*, London: Methuen, 1980, p. 167.

6. The available evidence is summarized in Martin C. Needler, "The Causality of the Latin American Coup d'Etat: Some Numbers, Some Speculations," in Steffen W. Schmidt and Gerald A. Dorfman, *Soldiers in Politics*, Los Altos, Calif.: Geron-X, 1974.

II

DEVELOPMENTAL
PERSPECTIVES

4

POLITICAL DEVELOPMENT

I

A great deal of insight into political processes has been added to our knowledge by the theory of political development, and it would not be correct to regard it merely as a fashion in political science that is now passé. It remains true nevertheless that political development theory was peculiarly the product of a specific era, and its genesis constitutes an interesting chapter in the sociology of knowledge.

That era, the 1950s and 1960s, was characterized by a particular configuration in international politics and by a particular stage in U.S. academic evolution, with some curious relations between the two dimensions. Scores of countries in Africa and Asia became independent, beginning in the late 1940s, as the European empires withered away, and the social sciences had to come to terms with platoons of new states governing territories that had hitherto been tucked into dusty corners of courses on imperialism and colonialism. The United States had meanwhile become a world power and had to adopt policies toward these new independent countries based on some conception of what U.S. interests were with respect to them.

Political development theory filled both of these gaps by providing generalizations about the society and politics of countries that were neither modern and industrialized nor ruled by Communist governments—the so-called "Third World." At the same time, it assigned the United States a role in relation to them by suggesting either that the processes of development would result in a country's coming to share characteristics with the United States and thus sympathizing with its attitudes and values, or else indicating in what way the United States could influence the process of development to ensure that a country would not become another Communist state.

Other factors influenced the creation of the theory of political development. One of them was the manifest success of economics. Being able to translate its concepts into formulas readily quantifiable in money terms, economics had been able to approximate the status of a science, understood as a cumulative body of propositions about the real world whose validity can be demonstrated with some rigor. The study of politics, in attempting to achieve the status of a science, naturally followed the lead of its sister social science, which had managed apparently to reconcile analysis and policy prescription in the emerging subfield of theory of economic development.

There was, curiously, another purely local factor giving impetus to the construction of a theory of political development heavily influenced by economics and aspiring to be both rigorous and policy-relevant. Massachusetts Institute of Technology, which specialized in the "hard" sciences and engineering, had decided to become a general university and was expanding its social science department. The social scientists recruited by the university were particularly eager to embark on the challenging enterprise of developing a new interdisciplinary subfield that, given the culture of M.I.T., could ensure the respect of their colleagues by being rigorous and quantitative while attracting government funding. In fact, scholars from M.I.T. took the lead in establishing the field of political development. In the early 1960s a joint Harvard-M.I.T. faculty seminar on political development, established by Samuel P. Huntington at Harvard and Myron Weiner at M.I.T., focused and stimulated much of the work being done in the field.[1]

The study of political development was a subfield in the social sciences, however, not a school of thought, and a variety of different approaches and conclusions were evident.

For many of the writers in the field, political development was not conceptualized as a process separate from social, psychological, or sometimes even economic development. For Walt Rostow, political development referred simply to the political changes that characteristically accompanied the various stages of economic development.[2] For Rostow, as for other writers who came to the study of development from economics, the process was a fairly simple, unidirectional one. Development meant the achievement of self-sustaining economic growth, that is, a continuous rise in national production. This required an increase in the rate of saving, the formation of capital, and a consequent rise in productivity. Rostow likened this, in a famous analogy, to the acceleration of an airplane that finally achieves takeoff.[3] Kenneth Organski's attempt to explain fascism in developmental terms also starts from economic premises.[4] Some years later Guillermo O'Donnell used a fairly complex economic argument in trying to account for the political evolution of Latin America. Like Organski's, his was not really a general theory, but one that tried to explain a specific phenomenon—the establishment of "bureaucratic-authoritarian" regimes in South Africa—on the basis of a specific set of economic circumstances, the supposed exhaustion of the possibilities of import substitution.[5]

In the early days of development theory, it was not altogether clear what process was being analyzed. One of the early books in the field, a multiauthored volume edited by Vera Micheles Dean, was entitled *The Nature of the Non-Western World*. It included a chapter on the Soviet Union along with those on Latin America, Africa, Southeast Asia, China, and the Middle East. From that perspective, the process under way was westernization, the acquiring by the rest of the world of the attitudes, values, and practices prevailing in Western Europe and North America. This was also the approach taken by the historian Cyril E. Black.[6] Although he wrote of modernization rather than westernization, to Black the process in question was one of the transmission at specific times of a complex of cultural traits, in much the same way as any cultural traits, such as growing corn or building round houses, are transmitted by contact among different peoples in the anthropologists' model. Thus modernity began with the beginnings of industrialization in Britain. It was transmitted, at various times, to British possessions overseas as these were colonized. Picked up by France, it was taken to Central and Eastern Europe with the Napoleonic conquests, and then to the French overseas empire.

To one of the most influential early writers, Daniel Lerner, the process of modernization was social and social-psychological, and was tied especially to improvement in communications, in the senses both of the transmission of information and of transportation, and especially to the spread of literacy.[7] In this model, traditional societies were penetrated by modern communications. Attitudes gradually changed, making people more open to the idea of change itself; their horizons widened to take in the entire world and all of its new possibilities, which included especially becoming literate and moving to the city.

II

The premise in most of this literature was that societies fell into three categories: traditional, transitional, and modern. Some scholars, especially those professionally concerned with the traditional societies, complained that lumping together in the same category exquisitely sophisticated societies such as that of imperial China with those of nomadic Bedouin or Central African forest dwellers was to overlook crucial differences.

Nevertheless, this paradigm seems the one generally accepted, implicitly if not explicitly. In the rather abstract field of public administration theory, Fred W. Riggs was concerned to distinguish the principal characteristics of traditional society from those of modern society, in the tradition of Max Weber.[8] Alex Inkeles and his associates tested their model of the social-psychological characteristics of modern men with a multinational opinion survey.[9] Lucian Pye surveyed his contemporaries' work on political development and concluded that the characteristics generally attributed to developed polities in the literature were constitutional stability, a high degree of participation, and role differentiation among public officials.[10]

Many writers, however, believed that the priority was to discern what was actually happening and induce generalizations from that, rather than to begin by constructing abstract models. In an important early article, Karl Deutsch pointed out that instead of looking for a single dimension in which change was taking place, one was forced to conclude after examining aggregate data that change seemed to occur simultaneously in a variety of dimensions: literacy, ownership of radios, rise in educational levels, rise in incomes, and political participation.[11] Deutsch proposed that all of these changes were in fact aspects of a single process, which he called "social mobilization." Gino Germani devoted a book to the description and analysis of this process, which he identified with modernization, with special reference to Argentina.[12]

The "first wave" of modernization and development theorists tended to be as optimistic as its formulations were imprecise. All of the indicators seemed to move together and to betoken improvement in the human condition. At the leading edge of a "second wave" of development theorists was Samuel P. Huntington, who pointed out that if development was possible, so was de-development, or, as he called it, "decay," while the constitutional stability characteristic of modern polities was, during the period of transition, actually threatened by the increase in political participation that took place.[13] At the same time, the present author was coming to similar conclusions with particular reference to Latin America.[14]

In fact, the ingenuous optimism of some early theorists of modernization and development helped to give the movement as a whole a bad name, as did the ethnocentrism of the authors whose model of the developed polity was a sort of idealized version of the United States.

III

While some authors have criticized individual assumptions or conclusions of development theory, others have gone further, in effect trying to turn the concept of development on its head.

The most striking expression of these views can be found in the writings of André Gunder Frank, who has taken the view that contact with Western Europe and North America, far from being a factor in beginning the process of development in the Third World, has actually had the opposite effect. Frank argues that in its relations with Africa and Latin America, the capitalist world has actually forced those areas to regress in their development, to abandon industries that would compete with those of the developed world and to become cheap-labor producers of agricultural and mineral products, with autonomous local governments having to give way to feeble puppet regimes. To underline the paradox, Frank refers to this process as the "development of underdevelopment." While some cases can be adduced in support of this view, such as the crushing by the British of the Indian textile industry, most observers believe that the facts do not support Frank's position as generally applicable in the Third World. A modified version has, however, found currency, especially in Latin America, in the guise of "dependency theory," which argues that the development of Third World countries has been distorted and limited by their dependence on the economically more powerful countries of North America and Western Europe.

While there is clearly a certain amount of merit to this view, it seems equally clear that the "dependency" of the Third World does not really constitute a special case. The world economy creates generalized interdependence, in which people in all societies are affected, often adversely, by self-interested decisions taken abroad. Political power is at times enlisted to do what economic power alone cannot. Even powerful countries like the United States may be subject to costly manipulation by an oil cartel or suffer the consequences of a computer-chip boycott. Those who are poor and weak, of course, suffer more.

The criticism made of dependency theory from a Marxist perspective, however, seems valid: that the emphasis on dependent *countries* being exploited by metropolitan *countries* is misplaced. Actually, multinational corporations, flying flags of convenience, whose corporate headquarters may be post office boxes in Vaduz or answering services in Nassau, whose stockholders may be the rich of Third World countries as well as people living in the developed lands, hold all of us to ransom in ways unknown to free-market theory. A serious attempt to come to grips with international political economy has to operate at a level of sophistication and complexity beyond that of dependency theory, however.

Although the elaboration of the theory of development seems now a lode that has been worked out, there is no doubt that its assumptions and conclusions still dominate ways of thinking about the Third World. Such concepts as modernization, development, and underdevelopment have become indispensable parts of our vocabulary. It is generally accepted that political development, understood as constitutional stability and democratic participation, is found more often in economically developed countries. And there seems general acceptance and absorption into the common sense of the study of politics that economic decline contributes to political decline; and that for transitional societies, which have left behind tradition without yet becoming modern, there is an inverse relation between stability and participation.[15]

NOTES

1. The author, who participated in the seminar during 1965–66, remembers looking around the room at Huntington, Weiner, Seymour Martin Lipset, Alex Inkeles, Gino Germani, Albert O. Hirschman, S. N. Eisenstadt, Lucian Pye, Everett Hagen, Fred Riggs, Kalman Silvert, Frank Bonilla, Hélio Jaguaribe, Frederick Frey, John Montgomery, Ithiel Pool, Dankwart Rustow, Ergun Ozbudun, and Ali Mazrui, and remarking to Michael Hudson that a bomb dropped on the room would be the end of the study of political development. In fact, several leaders in the field who were not present were also professors at M.I.T.: Daniel Lerner, Max Millikan, and Walt W. Rostow. Karl Deutsch, also a leader in the field, received his doctorate at M.I.T.

2. Walt W. Rostow, *Politics and the Stages of Growth*, Cambridge: Cambridge University Press, 1971.

3. A State Department officer stationed in Uruguay during the 1960s who was asked to describe the country's economy in terms of Rostow's analogy told the author that it was in the tailspin stage.

4. A. F. K. Organski, *The Stages of Political Development*, New York: Knopf, 1965.

5. Guillermo O'Donnell, *Modernization and Bureaucratic-Authoritarianism*, Berkeley: University of California Press, 1973.

6. Cyril E. Black, *The Dynamics of Modernization*, New York: Harper and Row, 1966.

7. Daniel Lerner, *The Passing of Traditional Society*, New York: Free Press, 1958.

8. Fred W. Riggs, *Administration in Developing Countries: The Theory of Prismatic Society*, Boston: Houghton Mifflin, 1964.

9. Alex Inkeles and David Smith, *Becoming Modern*, Cambridge, Mass.: Harvard University Press, 1974.

10. Lucian Pye, *Aspects of Political Development*, Boston: Little, Brown, 1966. My own reading of that literature finds agreement on the first two, but not the third, of those characteristics.

11. Karl W. Deutsch, "Social Mobilization and Political Development," *American Political Science Review*, September 1961.

12. Gino Germani, *Sociología de la Modernización*, Buenos Aires: Paidos, 1971.

13. Samuel P. Huntington, *Political Order in Changing Societies*, New Haven: Yale University Press, 1968.

14. Martin C. Needler, *Political Development in Latin America: Instability, Violence, and Evolutionary Change*, New York: Random House, 1968.

15. The fullest survey of the political development literature is Samuel P. Huntington and Jorge I. Domínguez, "Political Development," in Fred Greenstein and Nelson Polsby, eds., *Macropolitical Theory*, vol. 3 of the *Handbook of Political Science*, Reading, Mass.: Addison-Wesley, 1975.

5

POLITICAL ISSUES IN DEVELOPMENTAL PERSPECTIVE

I

One of the interesting outcomes of development theory has been the stimulus it has given to students of Western Europe to look at the old continent in a new light, that is, to reinterpret its history as a process of political development. The Norwegian scholar, Stein Rokkan, has played a major role in this development.[1] The ubiquitous Gabriel Almond has written in this area, as in many others. With Sidney Verba, he wrote a classic, although flawed, work based on opinion surveys in Mexico, the United States, and three Western European countries, measuring the extent to which the population showed the attitudes that the authors believed were appropriate to a developed polity.[2] With G. Bingham Powell, Almond treated political development as the meeting of a sequence of critical issues that face any polity—deciding such things as the form of government, the relation between center and local administrations, the relations of church and state, and the distribution of wealth.[3] The equally ubiquitous Seymour Martin Lipset, whose early writing asserted a correlation between political development, understood as democratic government, and economic development as indicated by per capita income,[4] went on to apply development theory to the United States in his study of the "first new nation."[5]

In general, the method of this "crises and sequences" literature has been to proceed inductively, generalizing what appeared to be the typical historical patterns. The issues that seemed to emerge in this kind of treatment of European history are, for example, the relations between church and state, the extension of suffrage, and the distribution of income. While this approach is unexceptionable as far as it goes, the difficulty is that it is incompletely generalized; that is, the kinds of issues that arose and the sequence in which they presented themselves seem to have been due in part to historical accidents of various kinds. This approach is really history, rather than political science. A more analytical approach, which uncovered an underlying logic in the process, would be more illuminating. Let us attempt such an approach here.

II

Two fundamental points should be acknowledged. The first is that all of the central issues that arise over time and serve to structure political conflict deal with the distribution and exercise of state power. That is, with the establishment of the state is created the capacity to make legitimate decisions binding the organized society. The critical question then becomes: To what set of persons and under what conditions is delegated the authority to exercise state power?

The second fundamental point is that the question of the distribution of wealth and income is not simply one issue that arises in turn in the sequence of critical issues along, for example, with the role of the church. Although the question of economic distribution may be more salient in connection with some issues than with others, it is an aspect of *all* disputes involving control of state power. Any issue that arises is considered in the light of what different solutions will mean for the power and well-being of different individuals, interests, and parties. Here we need to extend Aristotle's dictum that the distribution of power tends to follow the distribution of property; that is, the form of government depends on the manner in which wealth as distributed. A more comprehensive formulation would be that the normal equilibrium situation is for political power to be held by, or on behalf of, those who own the country's wealth and control the distribution of income. However, events may in the short term disturb this relationship so that there are for a short time separate economic and political elites rather than a single one. The congruence of the distributions of power and property can then be restored either by the holders of wealth's reasserting their control of political power, or by the holders of political power's decreeing a change in the distribution of property in their favor. The latter is what commonly occurs, as we have seen, following a revolution.

III

Logically, the state in its evolution can expect to face three fundamental issues, or deal with three major crises, each of which may have several aspects and various ramifications. These are the establishment of the state's autonomy, its internal structural definition, and its management of the succession (alternatively stated, the participation problem).

The first of these fundamental issues, the achievement of state autonomy, is critical in the initial establishment of the state. Physically, the state defines itself by establishing national boundaries. Politically, it defines itself by achieving independence from imperial control. Imperial control, it should be noted, is not limited to colonial rule from the metropolis of a foreign empire, as African states have recently established independence from British or French or Portuguese hegemony. In the case of the Catholic nation-states of Europe, the state also had to establish its autonomy from the asserted universal authority of the Catholic Church. For this reason, the conflict between church and state, so acute at some historical periods in European Catholic countries, can be regarded as analogous to the struggle of a newly independent state in Africa to eliminate the last vestiges of colonialism. Other issues, as we shall see, may have religious aspects, but the fundamental religious question in a Catholic country is that of state autonomy.

Although historically in Europe it has been the Catholic Church that has posed a threat to the autonomy of the state, other faiths with pretensions to control large areas of human behavior also threaten state autonomy. The founding of the Turkish state, the first modern country whose population was predominantly Muslim, required the adoption of a stringent anti-clerical policy. Israel, too, appears to be headed at the time of writing to a showdown between state and synagogue. The delicate balance of Israel's multi-party politics put the religious parties in the position of holding the balance of power on questions about which they felt strongly, compelling the postponement of the resolution of fundamental questions of state autonomy to govern important areas of human behavior.

The second question that must be faced by any state as it evolves is its own internal structure. That is, public authority must be allocated in two dimensions. The first relates the central government to subnational areas—states, regions, or provinces. The second and more important dimension is that of the relations among state organs at the national level: the two houses of the national legislature, perhaps, the head of state, the head of government, the courts, the permanent bureaucracy, and autonomous agencies. The question of the spatial distribution of power—that is, between the central government and the provinces—is particularly acute in the early days following the establishment of a new state because it seems to threaten the establishment of state boundaries that is part of the initial identification of state autonomy. If too much authority is devolved to the regions, it is felt, they might secede, thus threatening the basic premises of national identity. As time goes on and a national identity grows out of the shared experiences of an evolving national history, the possibility of secession normally declines.

IV

The allocation of authority among the various state organs at the national level is partly a question of constitutional theory and partly a question of existing tradition, as people tend to opt for institutional arrangements with which they are familiar. Nevertheless, the underlying questions here, as at times of other great national decisions, are those of power and the distribution of wealth. The various interests engaged in the political struggle assume that they will have more influence or control over one organ of government rather than another, so that the allocation of state authority has implications for the distribution of power and income.

In fact, future constitutional developments may prove them incorrect in these assumptions. The discussions that attended the writing of the United States Constitution illustrate this point. The conflicts over the allocation of powers were based largely on the assumption that the president would represent especially the most powerful national economic forces, the Senate would represent especially elite elements in the states, and the House of Representatives would represent those of lower social and economic status. These assumptions were based on the model with which the revolutionaries were most familiar, that of the monarchy, the House of Lords, and the House of Commons in the mother country. Moreover, those assumptions were to be validated by the electoral arrangements made. Only the House of Representatives was directly elected by the voters. The other powers were elected indirectly: the president by an electoral college, which was expected to consist of those economically, socially, and politically prominent in the life of the states, while senators were to be elected by the state legislatures. Now of course all of this changed as the idea of democracy spread and took firm hold. The contrast with Britain is instructive here. As democracy came to Britain, the franchise for the House of Commons was reformed and extended until the House became a democratically representative body. Meanwhile, power was steadily stripped away from the undemocratic monarchy and House of Lords. They seemed impossible to democratize, because the identity of the monarch and of the members of the Lords depended on birth and not election. (In fact, some categories of members of the House of Lords were not there automatically by birthright, and in more recent times proposals have been developed and partially implemented for a non-hereditary House of Lords.[6]) But the simplest and most direct way of making the government of Britain democratically accountable was to concentrate power in the elected House of Commons. In the United States, rights of birth did not enter, making it possible to reform the method of election of the Senate—first by action of the individual states and finally by amendment of the federal Constitution—so that U.S. senators would be directly elected. The electoral college for the presidency has remained but has become a formality of which most Americans are probably not even aware; for most purposes, the president is as though directly elected by the voters.

In fact, some presidents and some U.S. senators do represent the particular economic interests that the founders expected they would, partly for ideological reasons, and partly because money has come to play a major role in the system in the form of campaign contributions, fees for speaking engagements, and investment advice. The same effects are visible in the House of Representatives, however, whose members may be said to represent primarily the notables in their districts rather than those lower down the socioeconomic scale. It remains generally true, however, that disputes over the allocation of powers, although couched in constitutional-legal terms, are typically motivated by concerns over the impact of one resolution of the issue rather than another on the distribution of power and income.

V

The third critical issue in the evolution of modern states can be labelled differently: the regulation of the succession, the guaranteeing of equality of rights, or the extension of participation. Just as in a monarchy there are rules governing which of the possible claimants to the throne has the legitimate right to succeed (in Saudi Arabia the oldest brother, in Britain the oldest son, for example), in a representative constitutional state succession is determined by elections. Thus the critical question concerns who is entitled to vote.

In the countries of Western Europe, the right to vote for the lower house of the legislature was originally extended to those who qualified by owning property or enjoying an income of a specified magnitude. The number of qualified electors in a specific legislative district could thus be quite limited, perhaps even to a single individual. For elections to the legislature of the kingdom of Prussia voters were divided into three electoral colleges on the basis of how much they paid in taxes. In some districts a single individual constituted the entire uppermost electoral college.

The justification for limiting suffrage on the basis of property, income, or tax payments was that the country's business should be run like the business of a private company, and voting rights should depend on the size of one's investment. Of more direct concern was the fear that if those without property were to vote, their representatives would then be likely to pass legislation redistributing property, which was considered by the propertied classes to be a sort of legalized theft.

Nevertheless, property requirements for voting were steadily reduced and eventually eliminated altogether in all the Western European countries, and countries gaining their independence in the twentieth century have not stipulated property requirements for voting at all. Needless to say, the propertied classes were reluctant to extend the franchise, and in fact a democratized electorate has produced legislatures that have usually put through the redistributive policies they feared. Each extension of the suffrage, however, seemed preferable to the demonstrations and acts of violence, with their implied threat of revolution, that were being mounted by the proponents of electoral reform. As the British Labour Party politician, Tony Benn, put it, "The history of the British ruling class is the history of judicious retreats in the face of the inevitable. A mixture of realism, humanity, and laziness has saved them from the gallows and us from the barricades."[7] Following some British and French writers, Hélio Jaguaribe has written of three stages of democratic development: the democracy of the notables, the democracy of the middle classes, and the democracy of the masses. Jaguaribe found this evolutionary process to have existed in the history of ancient Athens and of twentieth-century Brazil as much as in nineteenth-century Europe.[8] Typically this process culminated in the extension of suffrage to all males—sometimes with exceptions such as those serving in the military or in prison, for example—over the age of 21, although in some instances a higher minimum age was stipulated for the electorate to the upper house of the legislature.

VI

Although universal manhood suffrage had thus been achieved—that is, barriers to political participation based on wealth had legally been removed—a further series of related critical issues remained to be resolved. The rationale for the extension of suffrage could only be the value of equality, the premise that all had a legitimate claim to equality of rights, unless it could be shown that some indisputably legitimate public purpose required their abridgement—as, for example, when someone is deprived of liberty as a punishment for crime adjudged in a court of law. The attainment of universal manhood suffrage, however, did not fully satisfy the implications of the principle of equality of worth for three reasons: It was not extended to women; it did not include rights other than suffrage except where being able to vote carried with it other rights, such as jury service; and it only considered men in their capacity as producers—as a Marxist would say, in their relation to the means of production—removing only disabilities imposed by reason of lack of wealth or income. The next set of issues to be faced in the development of the state implied, accordingly, the extension of rights not limited to those of suffrage to sets of people defined in ways other than as producers or possessors of wealth. This is the phase of development in which the countries of Western Europe and North America, and those in similar stages of development elsewhere, find themselves.

The most salient issue in this set is that of the rights of women. As recently as 1945, when the United Nations organization was established, in half of the member countries women still did not vote. Of course, the range of legal disabilities to which women have been subject is not limited to voting but includes such rights as ownership of property, access to employment, and equality in rates of pay.

Even where rights are legally guaranteed they may still be

denied in practice. This has especially been the case with racial minorities, and the civil rights movement in the United States, which reached one of its high points during the 1960s, is part of the drive toward the equality of rights for groups not defined in terms of economic class which is so characteristic of our present time. These groups, most of which are at the time of writing engaged in campaigns in the developed countries to secure more just treatment, include, along with those distinguished by race or gender, sexual deviants and members of linguistic minorities. Although they may be the same individuals or members of the same groups, the attempt by members of linguistic minorities to have their language accorded equal rights in the schools and in official use is analytically distinct from the struggle to remove legal disabilities from such groups as immigrants or racial minorities. If the linguistic minority is predominantly resident in a specific region of the country, the language-rights issue may be an aspect of a campaign for regional autonomy. It should not be confused, however, with issues of boundary demarcation and secession that were active at the time of the original establishment of the state, even though chauvinistic conservatives may oppose concessions to linguistic minorities by using the argument that the unity of the national state is under threat. Other noneconomic minorities whose rights are not always fully assured in Western Europe and North America and the attainment of which will therefore constitute political issues for the future are children, those accused of crime, that is, detainees and defendants, and prisoners, those convicted of crime and serving sentences.

Also belonging in this category as a group not defined by its status as producers is the general public in its role as consumers. The most important contemporary political movement seeking protection for the consumer is environmentalism. Western societies are not organized so that the environment is protected in the normal course of events without a special effort. Most participants in politics, through voting or other means, conceptualize themselves in the first place by their identity as producers, that is, as lawyers, steelworkers, or business managers. Consumers are supposed to protect themselves individually through their purchasing decisions in the context of an economic market. This means that one of the blind spots of the system is in the protection of public or "collective" goods such as clean air or water, which cannot be individually purchased.

NOTES

1. See Stein Rokkan, *Citizens, Elections, Parties*, Oslo: Universitetsforlaget, 1970.

2. Gabriel Almond and Sidney Verba, *The Civic Culture*, Boston: Little, Brown, 1965.

3. Gabriel Almond and G. Bingham Powell, *Comparative Politics: A Developmental Approach*, Boston: Little, Brown, 1966.

4. Seymour Martin Lipset, *Political Man: The Social Bases of Politics*, New York: Doubleday Anchor, 1963, pp. 27–63 (1st ed., 1960).

5. Seymour Martin Lipset, *The First New Nation*, New York: Basic Books, 1963.

6. Bishops of the Church of England, representative Scottish peers, and peers of first creation.

7. Tony Benn, "Reform in the Air," *Manchester Guardian Weekly*, April 16, 1964.

8. Hélio Jaguaribe et al., *Brasil—Sociedade Democratica*, Rio de Janeiro: Jose Olympio, 1985, pp. 435–36.

6

MILITARY RULE AND THE SINGLE-PARTY SYSTEM IN THE THIRD WORLD

I

In a recent article, Professor James Brown quotes General Kenan Evren, apparently with approval, as saying, "The Turkish Armed Forces are devoted to democracy and they are its indestructible guard."[1] One is glad to have this assurance from General Evren, since the point might otherwise not have been appreciated by those who were arrested, held without trial, and tortured by the military government he led, which seized power in 1980. But General Evren had tried to make the point clear at the time: "We have not eliminated democracy. I would particularly like to point out that we were forced to launch this operation in order to restore democracy with all its principles, to replace a malfunctioning democracy."[2] One need not doubt that General Evren was sincere in his sentiments, and, relative to other military forces that have seized power, the justifications given by the Turks may carry above-average plausibility. Thus Professor Brown's position is not as weak as that of some of his predecessors.

There are a surprising number of these defenders of military
seizures of power and interventions in politics in the Third
World. In the early years of African and Asian independence,
in the 1950s and 1960s, they were led by Lucian Pye, with
arguments to the effect that military officers could be expected
to be more patriotic and public-spirited than civilian politicians, more technically trained and modern in attitude, less
regionalist and ethnically chauvinist, and less corrupt.[3] All of
this is to accept military officers at their own valuation, in
keeping with their own self-perception—a sort of "official
story."

There are certainly noble clear-eyed soldiers who act hero-
ically without thought of self. I am not sure what proportion
of any given military body they constitute. I do know, however,
that the military ethic particularly lends itself to the construction of "official stories" that are not exactly the truth. Military
life requires unquestioning obedience to orders coming from
higher authorities that may not be familiar with local circumstances and conditions, to obey which may be difficult or impossible, or sometimes counterproductive; and yet not obeying
entails serious consequences. Politicians are known to lie; military officers, like lawyers, tend to reorganize the truth ret-
rospectively, to make behavior seem consistent with prescribed
legal norms. As a company clerk in the U.S. Army many years
ago, I did my share of creative writing to make the written
records show that things had indeed happened as they were
supposed to happen. Detailed investigation of the tangle of
personal and institutional motives occasioning a military seizure of power suggests that the picture of a disinterested patriotic military involving itself in politics without thought of
interest save that of the nation belongs to the same category
of literature.

The surprising feature of the existence of political scientists
who are apologists for military rule, however, is that military
rule is one form of the exercise of irresponsible and unchecked
power, and much of Western political thought has developed
precisely in order to find viable ways to prevent the exercise
of unchecked power. In extreme cases, it is true, military intervention can be brought under the category of tyrannicide or

the overthrow of an unjust ruler where no peaceful alternative to revolution is present. Even where such arguments can be made, however, they cannot be used to justify continued military rule past an interval necessary for the organization of elections and the return of the country to constitutional government. It misses the point to argue, as some have done, that military rule is able to achieve worthy goals, for example, by bypassing an obstructionist, corrupt, or reactionary parliament in order to achieve laudable goals of development or structural reorganization. In practice what this implies is the public's cooperating in the assumption by the military of absolute power and then *hoping* that such power is used for desirable purposes; in the absence of popular participation and legal controls, one can do no more than hope, however. This attitude represents a "triumph of hope over experience" far more dangerous than the case of the second marriage to which Samuel Johnson originally applied the phrase.

II

Nevertheless, the recent history of the countries of the Third World is in large part a history of military assumptions of power and military rule. A quarter-century of African independence has demonstrated that those who thought military intervention in Latin America had something to do with the Hispanic tradition were quite wrong. In Africa, except for a couple of surviving traditional monarchies (Morocco and Swaziland) and one or two surviving multi-party democracies (Botswana, and arguably Gambia and Sierra Leone), the only countries that have escaped military rule are those dominated by a single revolutionary party, very often still led by the nation's founding father, the hero of the independence movement. The single-party system thus seems to be, at least in part, an alternative to military rule, or at least it helps to immunize a country against military rule. What accounts for this phenomenon?

Simply put, military seizures of power are most likely when the incumbent government is regarded as illegitimate or ineffective, or both.[4] Military power rushes in to fill a vacuum of legitimacy or of effective government. The dominant single parties derive their legitimacy from their success in the revolutionary struggle against the colonial power or against the traditional exploiting class. Often the hero of independence himself continues at the head of the government. Moreover, the party itself provides the organizational basis and the personnel for the operation of government. There is no obvious vacuum there of either power or legitimacy. Continued poor performance, however, especially in respect to the economy, may erode the people's perception of the government as effective and even as legitimate, and a military seizure of power may then take place. The threshold to military intervention in this kind of single-party system, however, is much higher than in a multi-party system. It may succumb eventually, but it is likely to withstand a military takeover for a longer period, perhaps indefinitely.

The single-party system thus seems an especially resilient form of government. We can see its strengths and weaknesses clearly in the case of the oldest established single-party regime in the Third World, that of Mexico.

III

The single-party system of Mexico grew, like similar systems elsewhere, out of a successful revolution. The leader of the original revolution, Francisco Madero, was overthrown in a military coup, however, and the triumph of the revolution was not definitively established until after protracted fighting. Moreover, after Madero's death leadership of the revolution was contested by rival forces, which fought among themselves. Although the combat phase of the revolution was over by 1916, with the triumph of the forces loyal to Venustiano Carranza, no clear line of succession to supreme authority was established. A revolutionary tenet decreed that no president should serve more than one term. Accordingly, for the next 13 years fighting broke out anew every time a new president was to be picked. The revolution was finally institutionalized under the leadership of the outgoing president Plutarco Elías Calles in 1929 with the founding of the dominant single party, called today the Institutional Revolutionary Party (Partido Revolucionario Institucional), or PRI. The party has ruled continuously for 60 years, winning every election for president and (until 1989) for governor although opposition parties have won mayoralties and seats in the Chamber of Deputies and Senate. To be sure, on occasion, electoral returns for the presidency and governorships seem to have been falsified if it looked as though opposition candidates had a chance of winning. It is striking, however, how little—and for the most part, only how recently—rigging of elections was needed. For most of the period since the revolution, the government party was the choice of the great majority of the voters, and it is instructive to note the reasons.

In the first place, most of the country's significant political forces were included in the cartel that constituted the ruling party. In the early years, when armed conflict was a real possibility, these included those forces able to put troops in the field: the army itself, organized labor, and the organized peasantry. The armed intervention of labor battalions and peasant militias had been a decisive factor in the narrow victory of the government forces over an uprising in 1923. The loyalty of labor to the revolutionary regime was ensured by the conferring of the benefits of a progressive labor code, that of the peasant organizations by a land reform program.

Similarly, individuals were coopted by the conferring of benefits at the disposition of the government, especially government jobs. These were valuable in themselves, for their salaries and the career possibilities they contained, but also for the access they provided to illegal, but tolerated, self-enrichment. The provision that presidents could not be reelected meant that there would be a wholesale reshuffling of jobs every six years, at the conclusion of a president's term.

In addition, the expectation that the PRI would win elections and continue in office was self-reinforcing, as opportunists looking to make a political career naturally gravitated toward the party, along with anyone with goods or services to sell. The press has largely been kept supportive by the granting or withholding of authorization to purchase newsprint at below-market prices, along with various forms of indirect or even direct

bribery of journalists. Acceptance of the party was also
strengthened by the educational system, which glorified the
revolution and its heroes down to the current president of the
republic who is, at the same time, the leader of the revolutionary party.

The striking phenomenon, in fact, is not that the PRI has
remained in power, but that despite all the inducements to go
along with the PRI, opposition has nevertheless persisted and
grown. The primary basis for opposition seems to have been a
fundamental ideological commitment which has rendered the
individual immune to the blandishments of the PRI—Marxist
on the left, and Catholic on the right. Another source of opposition is the grievances of businessmen too small to have to
be placated and coopted by government, but too big to be ignored by PRI labor union leaders, who are sometimes racket-
eering gangster types.

There is, however, a lack of symmetry between the opposi-
tions to right and left of the PRI. The revolutionary rhetoric
used by PRI leaders, with its talk of the needs of the poor, the
grand reforms of the past, and the need for Mexico to assert
its national identity in the world arena, draws from the same
premises as the rhetoric of the left, and the left boundary of
the PRI is permeable, with some movement in and out, and
people of similar views being found on both sides of the line.
However, the PRI treats the major right-wing opposition party,
the Party of National Action (PAN), as a representative of those
forces defeated by the revolution: large landowners, the hyp-
ocritical clergymen who serve them, and foreign economic interests. The PAN is the PRI's favorite opposition, enabling it
to reassert its revolutionary credentials and drown out the
complaints of those who assert that the party has become cor-
rupted and conservative. Despite PRI's revolutionary rhetoric,
however, in the northern states where the PAN is strong the
PRI adopts positions on policy issues close to those of the PAN,
and there is movement of political candidates and their supporters across the line that divides the two parties.

In fact, the PRI is a party of integration that tries to maintain
the broadest possible appeal by coopting aspiring leaders of
minor parties and emergent interest groups and developing an

economic and social program that contains something for everyone. This strategy was eminently successful as long as the economy was booming and benefits for everyone could be financed. With the economic downturn that began at the end of the 1970s, however, that approach was no longer possible and policy became a matter of distributing economic hardship. Even these last terrible years of deprivation and suffering have, despite the predictions of a large proportion of the commentators, not brought to an end the hold of the PRI on the Mexican political system.

IV

Yet this institutional strength of the Mexican system is at the same time a sort of moral weakness. This is so because the best argument that can be made in favor of the single-party system is that it is transitional. Democracy needs an educated and enlightened citizenry, the argument goes. Where a population is illiterate and newly emerged from dictatorship, with no experience in participation in representative institutions, a case can then be made for a tutelary regime, which gradually creates representative institutions, expands universal schooling, and provides the economic minimum necessary before citizens can have enough peace of mind to devote their attention to political matters. As was noted in chapter 2, even as great an apostle of liberty as John Stuart Mill acknowledged that a "despotism" might be necessary as a transitional form until a fully representative government could be established.[5] Mexico at the initiation of the single-party system seemed perfectly qualified to fit that model. It was accustomed only to dictatorship, civil war, and military rule; a majority of the population lived in villages only imperfectly tied into the national communications networks; and most people's energies were absorbed in the struggle to survive.

The Mexico of today is quite different, however. Most of the population is literate, and higher education has expanded dramatically. The National University of Mexico, with over 100,000 students, is the world's largest, and 16 percent of the relevant age group are enrolled in institutions of higher education. A majority of the population is urban—in fact, Mexico City is the world's largest city. If the single-party system was meant to be transitional until an educated population prepared for political participation was created, then it has been successful in its task and should wither away.

But the single-party system has created interests dependent on its continuation, which resist a transition in the direction of multi-partyism despite the fact that pressures for greater openness have built up both within the party and outside it. Unwittingly, perhaps, President José López Portillo (1976–82) stated the situation correctly when he said: "There are only two alternatives. Either we continue to press onward in pursuit of our democratic vocation . . . or we shall find ourselves one day a replica of other regimes . . . those which use repression to insure arbitrary rule."[6]

The single-party systems of Africa find themselves in a particularly poignant situation. In addition to the reasons for a single-party system mentioned above, African regimes can add an especially powerful argument. Since the African states are, for the most part, arbitrary creations of the colonial era, whose boundaries do not coincide with ethnic demarcations, most countries contain two or more distinctive ethnic and language groups. National identity is recent and loyalties still attach primarily to the ethnic group and not to the modern nation-state.[7] Under these circumstances, in a multi-party system the different parties would not be likely to represent different programs, attempting to appeal to voters by rational exposition of their merits, but instead each party would represent a distinct ethnic group. What would be the merit of party competition under those circumstances? It would be all too likely to degenerate into tribal conflict and violence. In these circumstances, argue the apologists for the single-party system, the single party is able to transcend traditional tribal loyalties and to maintain the peace until the day national and not tribal identity will be the primary focus of loyalty. That at least is the justification given. Whether in reality the single party transcends ethnic loyalties, or instead becomes the vehicle for the domination of one ethnic group over the others, is an empirical question; in some African countries it is the former and in others the latter.

One of the lessons of the Mexican case is that for a single-party system to be acceptable to democrats, even as a necessary transitional form, there should be competition within the ruling party. In Mexico this has been provided by the existence of the affiliated organizations representing social sectors and subsectors that compete among themselves over the party's nominations to office and other benefits. In order to recruit new members, so that the size of their membership can be an argument for a greater share of the spoils of office, these organizations play an advocacy role on behalf of citizens with demands to make.

Another lesson from Mexico is that there should be freedom to dissent and to criticize, which helps prevent the massive errors to which an unchecked government is prone, contributes to educating the citizenry, and provides a base for an eventual multi-party system.

In fact, it is all too likely that the vested interests created by the political system will resist its transformation as the society develops to outgrow the justification for a transitional tutelary regime. The country's political life then becomes an expression of the clash between two principles of politics: the tendency of established interests to defend their positions of power, and the tendency of political systems to adapt to the requirements of changed social and economic circumstances. This is a recurring drama of human existence, one whose performance in the Soviet Union we are at present witnessing.

NOTES

1. James Brown, "The Military and Politics in Turkey," *Armed Forces and Society* 13(2), Winter 1987, p. 249.

2. Ibid., p. 242.

3. Lucian Pye, "Armies in the Process of Political Modernization," in John J. Johnson, ed., *The Role of the Military in Underdeveloped Countries*, Princeton: Princeton University Press, 1962.

4. I discuss this point at length in "Why the Military Leaves Power," *Harvard International Review* 8(6), May-June 1986.

5. The citation has been given as Note 7 to Chapter 2.

6. José López Portillo, "Informe," or State of the Union Message, September 1, 1980, distributed in the English version by the Mexican embassy in Washington.

7. For a detailed treatment of the issue, see Donald Rothchild and Victor A. Olorunsola, *State versus Ethnic Claims: African Policy Dilemmas*, Boulder: Westview Press, 1983.

III

POLITICAL
INFRASTRUCTURE

7

POLITICAL CULTURE

I

Culture consists of the patterns of learned behavior specific to members of a given society, and the values, attitudes, and modes of perception that these patterns of behavior reflect. There can be no doubt that culture in this sense exists and that the perceptions, attitudes, and behavior of a French woman in a particular situation will be different from those of a Russian in a similar situation, but in some respects like those of other French women. This is true in the political realm as in others. Nevertheless, there are very great difficulties involved in attempting to use political culture as an explanatory variable. Clearly, there are temptations to laziness and sloppiness in a political culture approach: "French politics works in this way because that's just how the French are." Moreover, if not used carefully, the political culture approach can become racist or ethnic stereotyping with a cover of social science jargon. What is clearly needed is the establishment of a solid empirical base for the assertion that specific attitudes do in fact constitute part of a given national political culture; otherwise, writing

about political culture may be imaginative and insightful but
may also be quite wrong.

A classic instance of misguided cultural explanation is that
of the explanation of the Tory working-class vote in Britain as
"deferential." The problem, which will be dealt with in a different context in Chapter 9, is the following: In Britain, the
Labour Party claims to represent the interests of the working
class and the Conservative Party represents primarily the interests of the middle class. There have traditionally been more
members of the working class, perhaps as much as twice as
many, as there are of the middle class, although the proportions
have recently begun to change. If all members of each class
voted for the party that claims to represent their interests,
then the Labour Party would win every election. In fact, however, the division of the vote between the two major parties
more often than not favors the Conservatives. Accordingly,
some members of the working class must be voting Conservative. Who are they? This is the problem of the Conservative,
or Tory, working-class vote.

Some observers, reviving an argument made toward the end
of the nineteenth century by Walter Bagehot, have put forward
the thesis that the phenomenon of the Tory workingman reflected a "deferential" component in British culture. Members
of the working class looked up to their social betters, it was
said, accepting their claims of social superiority at their face
value. A proportion of the working class voted therefore for
those they considered more entitled to rule rather than those
who would represent their own interests.

This theory won quite wide acceptance until, during the
1950s and 1960s, the results of attitude surveys showed that
the "deferential" voter in fact voted Labour as well as Conservative, and Tory working-class voters were primarily those who
were "cross-pressured." Such voters included, for example,
those in the upper working class whose possession of property
or higher incomes, or whose religious identification as members
of the Church of England, caused them to feel closer to the
Conservatives.

The opinion survey has thus made it possible to establish an
empirical base for statements about a country's political cul-

ture. In the absence of firm empirical evidence of this kind, one is best advised to explain political behavior as much as possible as the rational pursuit of self-interest, given the existing circumstances. If people do what it is in their interest to do, that is explanation enough, without the need of resorting to imaginative, but probably imaginary, hypotheses about culture.

Thus, for example, some writers have attempted to explain the dominance of two political parties in British history as reflecting an assumed British cultural addiction to sport; politics is said to be regarded as a team sport in which only two teams may participate. It is much more reasonable, however, before resorting to hypothetical cultural explanations of this type, to see instead whether the phenomenon cannot be plausibly explained on the basis of rational pursuit of self-interest, which in this case it indeed can. In the British single-member-district electoral system only one party can win the election; there are no consolation prizes. After knowledge of the electorate's preferences has been gained through a history of elections and/or public opinion polls, it will almost always become clear that at most two candidates can have a realistic hope of gaining a plurality of the vote. Accordingly, third and fourth parties will dwindle as their voters prefer to vote for the lesser evil, and as their leaders attempt to have more influence on policy and more promising political careers by entering one of the major parties. To be sure, on occasion one or more of the assumptions of this model may not hold good, and third or fourth parties may grow; we return to this topic in Chapter 8. Nevertheless, the rational self-interest model has a firmer foundation in logic and common knowledge, and is thus a starting point for refinement by further ratiocination and empirical testing preferable, for example, to the more nebulous and arbitrary sporting analogy.

II

Attempts at explanations of behavior based on political culture should thus create some empirical basis for assertions about cultural attitudes. This too is very slippery terrain, as can be illustrated by the example of one of the most influential

treatments of political culture—*The Civic Culture*, by Gabriel
Almond and Sidney Verba.[1] In the Almond and Verba model,
political culture in less developed countries embodied expectations that power would be used in an arbitrary, self-interested, and corrupt manner. The authors found, for example,
that in the United Kingdom only 7 percent of their respondents
expected that the bureaucracy would not treat them "as well
as anyone else," as compared with 9 percent each for Germany
and the United States, 13 percent for Italy, and a full 50 percent
for Mexico.[2] Responses asking about police behavior were similar. To say that different political cultures obtain in less and
more developed countries, however, embodies a logical fallacy.
The question asked about the respondent's expectations. Let
us suppose those expectations, instead of embodying culturally
determined attitudes, were simply factual statements reflecting actual experience with the behavior of the bureaucracy and
the police. All that the responses would then signify would be
that the bureaucracy and the police did indeed behave in a
certain way; that is, that in standards of official behavior the
country was either more or less developed. The causes for that
degree of underdevelopment or development, however, would
still remain obscure. They might be due to political culture, or
they might reflect other factors such as income levels, a point
which cannot be determined without further investigation. In
any case the response itself would not be indicative of a particular cultural attitude. A single individual traveling in all
of the countries discussed would also give different answers
with respect to the question of equal treatment by officials from
country to country.

A larger question, which the political culture approach seems
generally to have ignored, is: To what extent and under what
conditions do people's attitudes and values determine their behavior? It is clear, at one extreme, that authoritarian regimes
compel certain types of behavior regardless of people's attitudes. That is what makes them authoritarian. It seems in-
herently plausible, accordingly, that political culture
arguments are most appropriately made to account for different
behaviors among various democratic countries, and not differences between democratic and non-democratic countries. If it

is the nature of authoritarian regimes to use compulsion, why should one expect that under them behavior will reflect personal attitudes rather than the orders of the regime? It is thus possible that the attitudes of people living in an authoritarian system could be just as democratic as those living in a democratic system. It should not even be surprising to find, where the authoritarian regime is especially repressive and incompetent, attitudes that are even more pro-democratic than those of people living in democracies. Normally, of course, the regime would attempt to indoctrinate people with its ideology, and could have some success. But then the regime would cause the attitudes, and not the other way around.

III

In fact it seems a sort of calumny, an adding of insult to injury, to suppose that people live under dictatorial regimes because they actually prefer such regimes. That is nevertheless the view of a school of thought that seems to have gained wide acceptance. This view seeks to explain the relative lack of democratic practice in Latin America on the basis of an imputed non-democratic political culture. This presumed political culture is ascribed to Latin America's heritage from Spain, the principal colonial power. As one textbook puts it,

> A widely discussed determinant of Latin American political culture is the colonial heritage, manifested in the attitudes of the Latin American people toward both the decision-making role of government and their participation in it. The strong tendency toward personalism and authoritarianism in political culture is well known.... Political participation in the decision-making process means very little to average Latin Americans.[3]

This kind of statement is routinely made and routinely accepted in discussions of Latin American politics. And yet the approach it exemplifies rests on perhaps half a dozen undefended assumptions, several of which can be shown to be unjustified, the remainder being questionable.

One of the most serious difficulties is that referred to already, the implicit assumption that authoritarianism in the political system is a result of authoritarian attitudes. The causal relationship here must be demonstrated; it certainly cannot be assumed, since we know that people yearn for freedom *especially* when they live under authoritarian rule. Second, the tendency to authoritarianism in Latin American political culture, "well-known" though it may be, must still be shown to exist—and the opinion survey results appear to show that, contrary to expectations, it does not; that in fact, political attitudes in Latin American countries are pro-democratic.[4] But further difficulties remain. Why should a trait that was part of the colonial heritage necessarily survive until today? Many characteristics of the sixteenth century are no longer with us; why should this one be assumed not to have changed, without some empirical showing to the contrary?

And yet even the premise that the Spanish colonial heritage was particularly authoritarian, while plausible enough, would seem to require a vigorous defense. After all, authoritarianism was general everywhere in the sixteenth century—we seem to be dealing here with a *Zeitgeist* rather than a *Volksgeist*—not least in that England which English-speaking writers are wont to contrast with an alleged Spanish authoritarianism. James I of England regarded Spanish political thought as subversively democratic, and had the writings of Spain's leading political thinker, Francisco Suárez, burned by the public hangman. In the sixteenth century alone Henry VIII of England killed more religious heretics than did the Spanish Inquisition in its entire existence. The English "colonial heritage" included authoritarian Calvinism in New England and slaveholding in Virginia. It may be that the historical writing on Spanish authoritarianism in English still reflects the antagonism of the religious and national wars of the colonial period. The doctrine that the Spanish colonial heritage was particularly authoritarian for its age cannot just be assumed.

Moreover, one of the most obvious difficulties for the attempt to ascribe authoritarian practice in Latin America to an inherited Hispanic political culture is the fact that the most authoritarian countries of Latin America, over the years since independence, have been precisely the least Hispanic countries, those in which the proportion of Amerindians or Afro-Americans in the population is greatest.[5] The most purely Hispanic country in the region, Costa Rica, is also the least authoritarian. The reason for this is plain, and shows the marginal significance of political culture. Indians and blacks in Latin America were conquered or enslaved people, held in various forms of servitude, where the agricultural or resource base of the territory indicated that the path to wealth lay in the exploitation of labor in that manner. The political attitudes of the ruling groups in those societies were the ones appropriate to their social and economic position, just as the political attitudes of slaveowners in South Carolina reflected their social and economic position. What does cultural heritage have to do with this? Authoritarianism in Latin America seems to reflect not the attitudes of the many but the interests of the few.[6]

Accordingly, there seems little basis for accepting the thesis that authoritarianism in Latin America derives from authoritarian attitudes which themselves derive from an authoritarian Hispanic tradition—little basis in historical analysis, in comparative social analysis, or in contemporary public opinion. Of course, a specific democratic government may lose favor and be criticized, perhaps because of its economic performance, and the government that replaces it—which might be an authoritarian one—may inspire hope for economic improvement and enjoy a brief honeymoon on that account. It would be a careless observer indeed, however, who would interpret this phenomenon as a general preference for authoritarian governments growing out of ingrained cultural attitudes.

IV

Does all of this mean that the concept of political culture is quite without explanatory value? This is a difficult question to answer. It is certainly clear that different national cultures exist and influence behavior, yet the type of political regime in force, and its major features, seem not to be due to traits in these national cultures but instead to the course of major historical events, such as wars and depressions. Even where some kind of correlation is found between political regime and political attitudes, it is only too likely that attitudes are the dependent variable and that they change, through the mechanism of the reduction of cognitive dissonance, to become more appropriate to the regime, which in any case attempts to inculcate its norms and values into schoolchildren. Thus, for example, the Germans, if we include those both of East and West, have lived under five political regimes in the last 100 years. The character of the regimes changed due to defeat in war, economic collapse, and foreign occupation. After the Hitler experience and World War II, there were observers who thought it would be impossible to construct a democracy in Germany. Yet that has happened, and the "well-known" authoritarian values of Germans serve to buttress the democratic institutions of the Federal Republic, to the point that Almond and Verba take such attitudes to be components of an exemplary civic culture—although they would surely have found the same expectations of equal treatment by the police and bureaucracy in the old authoritarian imperial *Rechtsstaat*. Under the impact of external forces, Japan too has been reborn as a democracy, albeit with a culture as distinctive as it had under the empire.

Culture thus appears to affect style of behavior a great deal more than it does type of regime. Friedrich von Hayek captured the point when he wrote that he would not care to live in a totalitarian system, although an English or American totalitarianism would no doubt be milder than a German one. Perhaps there is something to be saved from the concept of political culture, but only if it is put on a firm empirical footing and only if it is clearly shown to what extent specific behaviors are shaped by specific attitudes.

NOTES

1. Gabriel Almond and Sidney Verba, *The Civic Culture: Political Attitudes and Democracy in Five Nations*, abridged ed., Boston: Little, Brown, 1965.

2. Ibid., p. 70. It may be thought superfluous to criticize the book since Almond and Verba themselves have disarmingly edited a book of such criticism, *The Civic Culture Revisited* (Boston: Little, Brown,

1974). The chapter in that book by Ann Craig and Wayne Cornelius contains a cogent critique of the methodology of the Mexican portion of the survey.

3. Russell H. Fitzgibbon and Julio A. Fernández, *Latin America: Political Culture and Development*, 2nd ed., Englewood Cliffs, N.J.: Prentice Hall, 1981, pp. 4–5.

4. See John Booth and Mitchell Seligson, "The Political Culture of Authoritarianism in Mexico: A Reexamination," *Latin American Research Review* 19(1), 1984; and Susan Tiano, "Authoritarianism and Political Culture in Argentina and Chile in the mid-1960's," *Latin American Research Review* 21(1), 1986.

5. Indeed, in the two least democratic countries, Haiti and Paraguay, a majority of the populations speaks neither Spanish nor Portuguese, but French Creole and Guaraní, respectively.

6. This subject is treated at greater length in the author's *The Problem of Democracy in Latin America*, Lexington, Mass.: D. C. Heath, 1987.

8

SOCIAL CLASS AND POLITICS

I

Very often, class is the most useful single category when one analyzes a political situation. Politics is about conflict and the management and resolution of conflict, and conflict does not take place without people's self-identification as belonging to competing groups. Membership in a social class is often the most important single factor in the process of self-identification. In stable developed countries, such as Britain, on which the present chapter will focus, political conflict takes the form of voting at elections. Class is usually the most significant single predictor of the party for which one votes. Clearly, it is not the only factor; the human qualities of individual candidates, and religious or ethnic identification, have a role to play. In fact, class has become a less significant predictor of the vote in recent elections, as we shall see. Nevertheless, it remains the most important one.

It may even be the case, as it is in Britain, that a major political party identifies itself overtly as the party of a specific social class: the name of the Labour Party is meant to identify the party as that of the working class. In the model of the class structure generally accepted in Britain, there is a very small upper class, consisting more or less of those with inherited titles and their families; a middle class of owners, managers, and professionals; and a working class of those who work with their hands, who are paid by the hour, whose jobs don't require higher education, and who, if they are men, don't need to wear a coat and tie.

Now several things need to be said about this extremely simple model. First, it is an urban-industrial model, uncomplicated by the need to embrace various categories of people working in agriculture, where the complexities of property and contractual relations, and fluctuating income levels, can make classification difficult. British governments came to the conclusion in the middle of the nineteenth century that Britain's destiny was to be an industrial power, and that the country would not be able to feed its own population but would have to import food. Although the livelihoods of Britain's remaining farmers are protected by legislation, which also restricts the urbanization of the countryside, those engaged in farming constitute only 2 or 3 percent of the British work force, and are an electoral factor only in a handful of districts.

A second peculiarity of this model is the continued existence of an upper class, although it is very small in numbers. This has the effect of confusing discourse a great deal since some very wealthy and powerful people are then considered to be members of the "middle" class. Moreover, the terminology has carried over to countries that do not have an upper class in the British sense of holders of hereditary titles. As a result, the person on the street in a country like the United States does not use terms referring to class in the same way as an academic sociologist, and endless confusions are generated. This can happen even in Britain, where the conclusions of a book on the middle-class voter were vitiated because the author confounded the "middle class," as understood above, with the class of people who are in the middle, that is, around the median, of a class-defined continuum.[1] The people "in the middle" of an array of all subclasses from top to bottom of the British social scale in terms of prestige and income would actually be the "lower middle class" and "upper working class"—that is, sales and clerical workers, owners of very small businesses, foremen, and skilled workers.

Despite a certain number of complications caused by factors such as preindustrial survivals, Britain is the country probably most transformed by the Industrial Revolution into an approximation of Marx's model of a two-class system in which the bourgeoisie is confronted by the proletariat; perhaps it is not accidental that Marx did most of his work in Britain. The situation is generally more complicated elsewhere, even in the developed world, by the presence of a larger agricultural sector, and often by the continuation in modified form of preindustrial forms of craft organization in the skilled trades, where the progression from apprentice to journeyman and then master craftsman status cannot be subsumed in a bourgeois/proletarian model. In West Germany, for example, instead of industrialization's leading to the abolition of the old craft system, new skilled trades characteristic of the industrial age, such as those of the electrician or beautician, have been organized along traditional craft lines.

But things are more complicated even in the simplest case, that of Britain. An observer interested in the phenomenon of class because it is a predictor of political behavior must confront the fact that many individuals do not identify themselves in class terms in the same way as the sociological observer. That is, there may be a distinction between an individual's class as perceived objectively and as perceived subjectively.

II

Objectively, then, what characteristics would be taken account of by a sociologist in deciding the class identity of a particular individual? First would be, in Marxist terminology, his relation to the means of production, that is, how he makes his living, and particularly whether he owns capital or whether the only things he owns from which he derives income are the hands with which he works. However, this contrast between capitalist and proletarian does not exhaust the varieties of occupation in a modern society, and sociologists normally group occupations into categories such as: owners—those who derive income from profits, dividends, interest, and rents; professionals; and managerial and technical staff. These categories constitute the upper- and middle-middle classes. Clerical and sales personnel, that is, workers in offices and stores, constitute the bulk of the lower-middle class. The upper-working class, sometimes called the "upper manual" category, consists of skilled workers and foremen. The "lower manual" set consists of unskilled workers. There is also a catch-all category for people who do not earn income directly, such as old-age pensioners, students, housewives, and the permanently unemployed. Clearly, there may be boundary problems in assigning any individual to a specific category: An office worker may be promoted through stages, so that it may not be always clear at what point the individual passed from the category of office worker to manager. Similarly, a crafts worker may become an artist and a skilled worker a technician. But of course there are boundary problems with any typology.

The greater difficulty is that criteria other than occupation may be relevant to perceptions of class, and the different criteria may conflict with each other, making class identification ambiguous. There is a sort of progression of such characteristics from those most closely related to occupational category to those related distantly or not at all, which the sociologist is likely to be most reluctant to take into account, but which may nevertheless be significant in determining the individual's class identity. Most closely related to occupation is income. In general, income tends to fall as one moves down the status hierarchy. However, this is not always the case, and just as a larger income may persuade a manual worker that he is in the middle class, a low income may cause a clerical worker to assign herself a working-class identity. This disparity between income and occupational status is most likely to occur at the border between lower-middle class and upper-working class, as anyone can attest who has recently paid a plumber's bill. Members of the middle class by occupation seem to be less likely to consider that lower incomes put them in the working class, however. Moreover, occupation may not predict an individual's subjective class identity if it is not in accord with his antecedents and family background. The university lecturer in sociology whose father was a manual laborer may still insist that he is working class, as will the trade union official now a member of the House of Lords. And one may work in a specific occupation only temporarily, even when "temporary" really means indefinitely, as when a waiter is "really" an actor waiting for a break or a writer trying to complete his first novel.

One of the major factors predisposing someone with a manual occupation to consider himself middle class in Britain is the ownership of a home, since the overwhelming majority of people in the working class have traditionally only been able to rent, frequently "council housing," that is, housing constructed by municipal authorities. One of the factors responsible for Mrs. Thatcher's retaining her position as prime minister for a second and then a third term was her policy, consistent with both party ideology and electoral advantage, of making it legally and financially feasible for renters of public housing to purchase their homes. Other factors that enter into a subjective class identity at variance with the one indicated by occupation are membership in a trade union, level of education completed, whether one has an appreciable amount of savings, and neighborhood of residence.

III

The difference between subjective and objective class goes a long way to solving what was for a long time a puzzle for analysts of British politics. The difficulty is this: If the Conservatives are primarily the party of the middle class and Labour the party of the working class, and if there are more members of the working class than there are members of the middle class, which seems self-evidently to be the case, then the Labour party should win every election. The fact that it doesn't implies that there must be members of the working class who nevertheless vote for the Conservative party. This is the problem of "the Tory workingman." Why would a member of the working class vote against his own interest?[2]

In the days before opinion surveys, a generally accepted explanation was that a portion of the working class voted "deferentially." They believed, that is, that only people of higher social status should properly rule. However, opinion surveys have shown that the amount of deferential voting among the working class is quite small and cannot by itself account for the problem of "the Tory workingman." Most significant explanations lie rather in two other directions: one, that many people who might be considered working class by the sociologists in fact identify subjectively as middle class; and two, that some voters choose the Conservatives as the party, not specifically of the middle class, but more generally of "the Establishment." The Conservatives, that is, are also identified with certain traditional religious and national symbols as well as with a class position on domestic policy. The Conservatives are the party of the established Church of England; as one wag put it, the Church of England is the Conservative party at prayer. Thus working-class Anglicans may vote Conservative on that basis. The Conservatives are also the party of the flag, of "king and country," that is, of national chauvinism, and are thus the party of those who favor "a strong defense," military solutions to international problems, and an unwelcoming attitude to foreigners, at home or abroad. In extending the franchise, the great Conservative leader Benjamin Disraeli was betting not only on deference but also on the national chauvinism that could attach a segment of the working class to the party of empire. It was in this tradition that Margaret Thatcher prosecuted the war with Argentina over the Falkland Islands in 1982, and her party benefited from it electorally the following year. Some additional factors help to account for the phenomenon of the Tory working-class voter, such as a slight tendency for people's attitudes to become more conservative as they grow older. Even when account has been taken of all of these sources of deviation from an electoral choice determined simply by objectively defined class position, however, it remains true that class is the single most important predictor of partisan choice.

IV

Of course, class in this sense is a product of conditions in Europe in a given historical period, and students of non-industrial Third World societies must beware of importing European notions of class into such situations. In much of rural Africa, in the island societies of the Pacific, and in parts of Asia, production is organized on the basis of the extended family. In what might be regarded as the modal type, perhaps the purest surviving case today, the society of Western Samoa, the extended family structure has been built into the modern state, so that only the heads of the extended family, the *mataes*, vote in elections for the parliament. One should beware of romanticizing this situation and assuming that because family rather than class is the key organizing principle, then exploitation does not exist. In the traditional Pacific societies exploitation is quite acute, in fact, with privilege and work obligations structured by sex, age, and birth order. Children above the age of seven and unmarried teenagers and youth are expected to work hardest, be fed last (if the food has not run out), and answer back least. Thus outwardly idyllic societies may conceal a great deal of teenage depression, alienation, and even suicide.

Although under modern European conditions the class system is most compatible with a society based on the nuclear, rather than the extended, family, with individuals free to find their level in the social class system based on their own occupations and related characteristics—although family background remains a factor—at some stages of evolution the extended family system seems to be compatible with a class structuring of society. Fustel de Coulanges has ascribed the origin of the patrician and plebian classes of ancient Rome to circumstances in which an extended family, the original occupants of an extension of agricultural land, acquired dependents and clients from families of immigrants, prisoners of war, disinherited minor branches of other families, and the like.[3]

The European class system is in part the residuum of waves of immigration, conquest, and religious strife, but is primarily today the product of the industrial and commercial organization of our time. How is it destined to change as the economic processes of our time change? What will the class system of the postindustrial era be like? While too many imponderables enter for any firm predictions to be made, some changes have already begun to occur that will likely continue and grow over time. One of these is the blurring of the line between working class and middle class as the range develops of occupations that lie clearly neither on one side nor the other of the traditional class division. Many scientific and technical vocations have come into existence whose occupants seem more than skilled manual workers but less than professionals. Harold Wilson, who served as British prime minister in the 1960s and 1970s, attempted with some success to get the Labour Party identified as the party of science in order to appeal to this socially ambiguous new element. Ironically, Margaret Thatcher, the daughter of a grocer, was herself an industrial chemist before deciding to change careers and study law.

Some other curious developments should be noted here. One is that as Europe has become more affluent, an upgrading of skills and status has occurred so that many jobs at the bottom of the prestige hierarchy have been left open and have been filled by immigrants, often of darker skin color: West Indians in Britain, North Africans in France, Turks and Portuguese in West Germany, Italians in Switzerland. Questions of class have become entangled with questions of cultural and linguistic rights and indeed with racial prejudice.

More recently, the natural capitalist process of the replacement of labor by machinery, accelerated by heightened competition within the European Common Market, and with Japan and the newly industrializing countries of East Asia, and intensified by the monetarist backlash against rapid inflation, has led to the apparent acceptance of large-scale structural unemployment as a permanent feature of the scene. Some people have argued that in Western Europe and the United States many young people, especially those of darker color resident in inner cities, may never achieve regular permanent employment. Extrapolating this situation, one can arrive at a vision of the society of the future in which the affluent live surrounded by high walls and armed guards to protect them from the marauding of an internal barbarian class, just as the external barbarians harassed the margins of the Roman empire. An alternative scenario, however, is that governments that follow more egalitarian welfare policies will achieve an integration of those who are today marginal in a high technology society where the status distinctions between different kinds of work have been softened, if not eliminated.

NOTES

1. John Bonham, *The Middle Class Vote*, London: Faber, 1954.

2. The problem of "the Tory workingman" has been examined in Allan Silver and Robert McKenzie, *Angels in Marble*, London: Heinemann, 1968; and Eric Nordlinger, *The Working Class Tories*, Berkeley and Los Angeles: University of California Press, 1967.

3. Numa Denis Fustel de Coulanges, *The Ancient City*, translated by Willard Small, New York: Doubleday Anchor, 1955 (originally published 1864).

9

THE TWO-PARTY SYSTEM

I

The political party is central to the way in which democratic politics is structured today. A well-functioning political party recruits potential candidates for office and selects from among them. It organizes policy alternatives into a program that enables the voter to choose among alternative futures for his country. In opposition, the political party criticizes the government in power, inhibiting it from abusing its position or straying too far from generally acceptable policies, and in so doing educating the voter. At least, this is what a political party does in the model of a well-functioning democratic political system.

In structuring political conflict the political party itself may become a basic point of reference for the individual. That is, political party loyalties are often inherited, so that, instead of choosing a party whose views are closest to her own, the voter may instead adopt the views of the party into which she was born. As W. S. Gilbert put it,

> Every little boy or gal
> That's born into the world alive
> Is either a little Liberal
> Or else a little Conservative.

Nevertheless, people do switch parties. They stay with the inherited party so long as the characteristics predisposing them
to favor it, principally social class and religious belief, remain
the same. If those characteristics change, then party loyalty
itself may change. This implies long-term shifts in support from
party to party.

But shifts in the vote for parties and candidates occur on a
short-term basis too, in fact from election to election. Such
shifts are due not only to changes of permanent loyalty from
one party to another, to changes in the composition of the electorate as some voters die and are replaced by those qualified
to vote for the first time, to previous voters failing to vote and
previous non-voters deciding to go to the polls, but also to shifts
in voting choice by voters not firmly committed to one party
or another but available to change depending on the way they
see the issues or candidates at each election. Since it may well
be their decision that determines the outcome of the election,
clearly these "floating" voters are critically important and the
party or candidate acting rationally so as to win election must
pay special attention to their preferences. Who are they?

It would be nice to think that voters who shift their choice
from one election to another are sturdy and conscientious in-
dependents who carefully weigh the issues and examine the
candidates before deciding what the public interest requires,
and indeed here and there a civics textbook may draw such a
picture of the uncommitted voter. It is, however, all too likely
that an informed voter who understands his own interests, who
follows the news and has a well-developed conception of where
the public interest lies, will long since have decided what the
different partisan options signify, and will be committed to one
party banner or another. The surveys suggest that floating
voters are likely to be less well informed and less interested
in politics than committed partisans. They may also be voters
who are cross-pressured or of ambiguous social identification.

That is, if fundamentalist Protestants vote predominantly Republican, let us say, and union members predominantly Democratic, then a fundamentalist union member may be pulled in two directions. If more prosperous members of the middle class vote Conservative and the poor members of the working class Labour, then an underpaid office worker or a prosperous plumber may be unsure as to where his or her loyalties belong.

Of course, these various social identities and economic categories become of relevance to the electoral process as they are translated into policy preferences. The prosperous plumber may worry about high taxes and thus may opt for the Conservatives as the party identified with lower tax rates. However, if economic activity is declining and unemployment rising, he may instead choose the Labour party as the party more likely to maintain a high level of employment.

II

If one conceives of the range of policies on economic and social issues that a party can take as ranged on a continuum from left to right, then the policies located on the right side of the spectrum will be those more favorable to business, the wealthy, and the interests of capital, while those on the left will be more favorable to labor and the poorer members of society. A left-wing policy would be one that taxed more heavily those with higher wealth or income in order to create social programs that benefited those lower down on the income scale.

One of the most widely accepted principles of comparative politics theory is that in a two-party system, given certain assumptions, the two parties will take up policy positions toward the center of the spectrum. The reason for this is that each party can take for granted the votes of its natural followers to either side of the political spectrum, but they must compete for the decisive vote of the undecided in the center. As a result, party programs are likely to be moderate and ambiguous, and to resemble each other in their major features.[1]

This general principle is always resented and disputed by more extreme partisans, who argue that in order to win the party must present a distinct image different from that of the other party; otherwise it risks losing the vote of its natural adherents, who may simply stay home on election day rather than vote for a leadership of spineless opportunists that has forgotten or ignored the party's principles. Experience shows that the moderate leadership normally has the better of the argument, however. The party's dedicated militants will, in the last analysis, however much they grumble, prove loyal and vote for the party, since even under its moderate leadership it represents the better of the two alternatives—at a minimum, the lesser of the two evils.

Moreover, even if some militants stay home on election day, the vote of a moderate in the center is worth more than the vote of a disaffected militant who abstains. A centrist voter who is recruited means not only the addition of one vote, but the loss of that vote to the other party; in other words, it is worth twice as much in the election as the vote of a militant abstainer, which is lost but is not added to the vote total of the opposition. Normally, accordingly, the parties in a two-party system take moderate and centrist positions on policy questions.

When this does not occur one has to specify the assumptions of the model on which the prediction was based and see which of those assumptions did not hold true. This illustrates the value of a logical model in the social sciences. What is important is not only the predictions about behavior it produces, but the logic of the causality it imputes to that behavior, and the assumptions it specifies. When a prediction based on the model proves false, then an examination of the situation in the light of those assumptions can help to pinpoint which of the assumptions did not hold good and thus can indicate the reason for the unanticipated outcome.

In the case of the model of competition in a two-party system, with its conclusion that party positions will be located toward the center of the spectrum, the following assumptions are made:

1. A single dimension of policy is the only, or the overridingly important, one. Clearly, this assumption will not always hold. In some cases, for example, foreign policy questions may be of importance, and a person's position with respect to them

may not correspond to her position on the social/economic dimension; that is, not everyone who is center-right on the economic dimension will be at the same point on a foreign affairs spectrum, even if one could be constructed.

2. The various social and economic issues can be summed into a single scale. This assumption generally holds pretty well. A person's position on social welfare spending, for example, will normally predict his position on taxes, inflation, and unemployment. In the present state of our thinking about economic policy, most people who favor greater spending for social welfare purposes accept the likelihood that greater taxes will be necessary to pay for that spending. They prefer the tax burden to fall more heavily on those most able to pay, and they also desire government policies that promote full employment, even if the higher rate of economic activity implied may lead to a higher rate of inflation.

These views normally go together because they reflect the underlying economic position of the person holding them. She is a worker, employed or unemployed, in the lower half of the income distribution, for whom the possibility of losing her job is real, and who would stand to benefit more from government social spending than she would have to pay in taxes to finance such spending. (Alternatively, she is a member of the middle class who sympathizes with such persons.) Toward the other end of the policy spectrum one finds recipients of higher incomes, who are less in need of government social services because they can pay for their own requirements, but are afraid they will be taxed for such services. They are concerned not about losing their jobs, but about the erosion in the value of their savings and investments if inflation gets out of hand. Thus the summation of the major social and economic issues in a single scale of this kind appears quite feasible.

3. A model of this kind also assumes that voters are informed about their own interests and about the positions on policy questions of the parties and candidates, and that they vote rationally in terms of those interests. Clearly, there are problems with respect to these assumptions, and the extent to which the assumptions correspond to reality will vary at different

times. It remains true, however, that voters are more likely to choose rationally in keeping with their economic interests than they are, let us say, on foreign policy questions, whose remoteness from immediate personal interests often means that the voters' choices are predominantly symbolic ways of securing emotional gratification, whether these are based on fantasies of self-assertion and revenge, or sweet dreams of love and brotherhood.

Although the technicalities of economic policy may be beyond the grasp of many voters, most voters have a stereotyped image of each party's economic orientation that serves just as well. Ironically, the voter may have to depend more on his stereotyped image of the parties' positions the more the two parties' views, as expressed in their election rhetoric, resemble each other. And he may not be deceived. Thus, for example, while no party runs on a program of promoting unemployment, the surveys show that voters in Britain consider that unemployment is likely to be higher under Conservative governments, and voters in the United States, under the Republicans. In fact, the data confirm these expectations. After the heights reached by unemployment figures in Britain during the 1930s under Conservative governments, it became until the 1980s a maxim that no government could politically afford to let unemployment rise above the one million mark; in fact, under Margaret Thatcher unemployment passed three million. Since World War II, annual rates of growth in employment in the United States have always averaged over 2.5 percent under Democratic presidents and always under 2 percent for Republican presidents.[2]

4. The final major assumption is that party leaders act so as to win elections by maximizing votes. This assumption, too, may not hold. In fact, some party leaders would indignantly reject this characterization of their behavior, calling it appropriate only for unprincipled opportunists. Mrs. Thatcher has made this point by referring to herself as a "conviction politician" rather than a "consensus politician." Nevertheless, most party leaders most of the time consider that they can only achieve their objectives if they hold power. Thus their behavior must be such as to achieve

power, even where this requires some modification in the party's stance on question of program.

As we noted, Margaret Thatcher has made plain that she does not behave as the model of rational action requires that she does, and yet she has been the most successful British politician of the twentieth century in electoral terms, winning three general elections in succession and serving a longer continuous period as prime minister than anyone else. She has not moved the Conservative party program to the center of the spectrum, but instead has maintained it at a point much further right, cutting social programs and allowing unemployment to rise. Thus some assumptions of the model must not have held; by examining the model's assumptions in reference to recent British politics we can then identify the reasons for Mrs. Thatcher's success.

III

The first assumption not to have held is that of the single salient dimension of policy. Along with undistinguished performance, not to say failure, in economic terms, Mrs. Thatcher had a signal success in foreign policy in the eyes of British voters. This was the victory over Argentina in the war growing out of the Argentine occupation of the Falkland Islands. This military victory gave the British an unusual opportunity to feel pride in their nationality; the fact that it was a victory in response to an aggressive act by a military dictatorship with an unsavory human rights record evoked gratifying memories of Britain's "finest hour" in World War II. There was also a carry-over in positive appraisals of Mrs. Thatcher, whose self-willed obstinacy now came to look more like Churchillian determination.

More importantly, the Conservative failure to act rationally in terms of the model so as to maximize votes happened to occur at the same time as similar behavior on the part of the Labour leadership. Shortly after Mrs. Thatcher became Conservative leader and prime minister, the Labour party chose a leader and a program clearly on the left, taking up a position on issues not favored by centrist opinion in Britain in three respects. The party pledged (with some qualifications) to withdraw Britain from the European Economic Community, to resume the nationalization of industry, and to abandon nuclear weapons unilaterally. If one party leadership acts irrationally, in terms of the model, by locating its programmatic position much to one side of the center point, then the other party's leadership can pick up support by moving its party position. For example, as Mrs. Thatcher moved her party's views to the right, opportunistic Labour leaders could have taken their party further right, still maintaining a distance between their position and that of the Conservatives but picking up the votes of those unwilling to go along with Thatcherism. Instead, the Labour party moved the party program further to the left, leaving many centrist voters unhappy with both major parties. This created the policy space for the emergence of a third party, which indeed was founded: the Social Democratic Party. The SDP originated in a split-off by some leaders of Labour, alienated especially over the decision to withdraw from the European Community and over changes in the party's rules that favored the left wing in leadership selection.

The Conservative party did not split, partly because it was in office. That is, Mrs. Thatcher's tactics seemed to be successful, and dissidents could be coopted, at least in the early years of Mrs. Thatcher's premiership, by being given office. In addition, disloyalty to a serving prime minister is more serious than to a leader of the opposition. Moreover, the issues on which Tory dissidents differed from Mrs. Thatcher were continuous ones; that is, the differences were questions of degree. Differences within the Labour party, however, were discontinuous. Although under the leadership of Harold Wilson the Labour party had managed to patch up ambiguous formulas on Europe, the question was really a discontinuous one: to stay or to withdraw. The nationalization of industry was the same kind of issue.

Thus one can see that although a model of rational action may serve to predict behavior fairly well, it is equally helpful when its predictions are not borne out because it is structured in such a way, when the critical assumptions are specified, as to afford an explanation of the causal factors at work.

IV

The model we have just been discussing is that of competition in a two-party system. A logical prior question asks why there should be only two dominant parties. After all, people's views can be distributed into more than two schools of thought even on a single issue, and politics deals with many issues. Surely a multiplicity of parties is necessary to give adequate representation to the voters' opinions.

Any analysis of a party system must begin with an analysis of the society whose divisions it reflects. It is true that the dominant cleavage in British society is between middle class and working class. Moreover, important secondary cleavages do not cut across class divisions, but rather reinforce them. The Church of England is heavily middle class, for example; speakers of Welsh are predominantly working class. Thus a two-party system does not seem to falsify Britain's social realities.

Yet in fact Britain during the twentieth century has always had more than two parties; it is just that the electoral system is such that two parties share most of the House of Commons seats. To win more than a handful of seats a party needs to command over 30 percent of the national vote. This follows from the logic of the electoral system, which in Britain as in the United States is that each district elects the one person who receives the most votes. In this "Anglo-Saxon" system it is not necessary that the winning candidate receive 50 percent of the vote, so no runoff is required.

Under conditions of free competition a variety of different parties contest the elections, but the deck is stacked against third parties. In the elections of June 1987 the Liberal–Social Democratic Alliance received 23 percent of the vote but only 6 percent of the House of Commons seats. In the long run, two parties at most can reasonably expect to be able to win a majority of seats in the legislature or a majority of votes in each electoral district. The voters for third and fourth parties tend to become discouraged when they cannot win seats; why "waste" your vote? By contrast, electoral systems constructed along proportional lines tend to encourage a multiplicity of parties, since even minor parties can hope to elect members and thus exert an influence in the making of policy.

Thus it appears that the electoral system has a direct causal relation to the number of political parties of significance that function within a system. Some observers have rejected this argument, however, arguing instead that the causal relationship lies in the other direction; that in fact electoral laws are not conceived immaculately but are the product of a specific majority party, or majority coalition of parties, which drafts a law that will favor its interests. Thus, instead of the number of political parties and their character being an effect of the electoral law, it is instead a cause of the electoral law. This point has been urged, for example, in a sophisticated argument by Leslie Lipson.[3]

The point is perfectly well taken. Historically, in many countries electoral laws were passed by parties that expected to do well out of them; elsewhere traditional election laws are maintained by parties they favor. However, Lipson's argument does not refute the causal connection that goes from electoral system to party system; in fact it assumes it. If a particular party or coalition of parties adopts an electoral law because it will be favored by that law, then that means they acknowledge that the electoral law has a causal role in determining the party system. That's what it means to say that a party will be favored by the law. *Historically*, the "cause" of a particular electoral system may be that it was imposed by parties that stood to benefit from it, but *logically* the causal influence of electoral system on party system remains as we have stated it. As can be seen from this example, historical modes of explanation do not eliminate the necessity for an understanding of the logic of social causation, but rather require such an understanding if they are to make sense.

NOTES

1. Anthony Downs, *An Economic Theory of Democracy*, New York: Harper and Row, 1957, elaborates this logic in its most exact form, but the general point was part of the folklore of political science long

before. Before Downs's work, the source most commonly cited on this point was probably E. E. Schattschneider, *Party Government*, New York: Rinehart, 1942.

2. The actual figures are Truman, 2.74; Kennedy and Johnson, 2.73; Carter, 3.3; Eisenhower, 1.32; Nixon and Ford, 1.97; Reagan, 1.56. Victor Perlo, "Job-Growth Rate under Reagan is Down," letter to the editor, *New York Times*, June 28, 1986, p. 14.

3. Leslie Lipson, *The Democratic Civilization*, New York: Oxford University Press, 1964, pp. 337–38. The current state of the literature on this question is surveyed in Richard Gunther, "Electoral Systems, Party Systems, and Elites: the Case of Spain," *American Political Science Review* 83(2), September 1989, pp. 835–36.

IV

POLITICAL
INSTITUTIONS

10

PRESSURE GROUPS, BUREAUCRATS, AND POLICYMAKING

I

The most recent literature on policymaking by governments in advanced industrial societies has focused on whether the process is most adequately characterized as pluralist or corporatist. The pluralist model envisions a sort of free market of pressures on government decision-makers, in which a variety of interest groups exert themselves to bring influence to bear at different points of the decision-making structure, their levels of interest and modes of operating varying with circumstances and the nature of the issue involved. In the corporatist model, specific interest groups, whose membership may be universal and even compulsory for the category they represent, have a recognized status and guaranteed access to the decision-making process.[1] In Britain, for example, heads of departments are sometimes required by statute to consult with advisory bodies consisting of representatives of specific interests affected by the activities of the department before making certain kinds of decisions. Thus before setting support prices for farm products, in the days before British membership in the European

Economic Community transferred that function to Brussels,
the British minister of agriculture was obliged to consult with
representatives of specified farmers' organizations. As far as
Britain is concerned, the most appropriate formulation based
on the current state of the debate seems to be that neither
corporatist nor pluralist models adequately capture the reality.
Rather, elements of both are present, and the relative weight
of each mode of patterning pressure group–government relations varies depending on which party, and which leaders, are
in power.[2]

However, two major questions are assumed away by the formulation of the issue as the pluralist model versus the corporatist model. They are, first, the question of how much effect
outside pressures of any kind have on government decision-
making—that is, the question of how autonomous the state is;
and second, the question of whether decisions made, and pressures brought to bear, have to do only with minor or marginal
issues, while the more fundamental questions of public policy
have already been determined by some overriding power relationship such as the hegemony of a specific social class, the
predominance of a foreign power, or the requirements of the
prevailing international economic system.

II

Liberal democratic theory seems always to have underesti-
mated the autonomy of the state, that is, the independent decision-making role of elected office-holders and career officials.
In democratic theory government should represent the popular
will, while career civil servants operate at the direction of an
elected executive, implementing laws passed by elected legislators. If the people are not vigilant, then "special interests"
may come to wield undue influence in the process. In point of
fact, however, presidents and prime ministers may have a great
deal of room to maneuver. With respect to many issues, public
opinion will not have crystallized, and may be willing to follow
the decision-maker rather than to lead him. On many questions
the balance of contending interests may be such that no single

course of action has a preponderant weight of interest behind it.

There are indeed some British traditionalists who espouse an alternative model of policymaking in which the state is almost completely autonomous.[3] In this model the voters choose a government team on the basis of its skills and abilities, rather than its views; the Crown's ministers and civil servants take public opinion into account, but make decisions on their own best judgment as to the public interest.

Now of course this model, like the liberal democratic model in which government simply reflects the will of the people, is an idealized and partial version of reality. It is certainly true that in any governmental apparatus can be found devoted public servants who loyally and in a disinterested manner advance the cause of the public interest as they see it. It is nevertheless regrettably true that for most permanent government officials the public interest is conceptualized in such a way as to coincide with the interest of the civil service as a whole, with that of the individual's own bureau in particular, and indeed with the personal and career interests of the individual bureaucrat himself. In part, that is, the bureaucrat necessarily believes in the importance of his own work and thus acts in the name of a partial and even distorted view of the public interest. His invocations of the public interest may even be quite hollow, and his operating motives may be restricted to protecting his own turf, expanding his share of the budget and his authority, promoting his career, or even merely trying to avoid giving offense so as not to prejudice his chances of surviving on the payroll until he becomes eligible for a pension.[4] For a good part of the time, there is no conflict among the behaviors mandated by the different motivations. Sometimes, however, there is and one can distinguish, for example, between a pattern of bureaucratic behavior characterized by caution, inertia, and reluctance to depart from established routines, even when they may have lost their original purpose or even become counterproductive, on the one hand, and, on the other, an assertive, manipulative style of bureaucratic politicking. The point for our present purposes is that the outcomes of the policymaking process may be explicable only on the basis of considerations specific to the personnel who staff the bureaucracy, rather than those embodied in models of popular control of government or the pressures of outside interest groups.

III

Especially in countries of the less developed world, but in smaller and weaker countries generally, it is often the case that the country's processes of making policy are conditioned by a general awareness of the importance of good relations with the hegemonic power. Policymakers in the Dominican Republic, for example, may have perfect freedom of action in a formal sense; however, they realize that, given the dependent condition of the country's economy, U.S. sugar purchases or tourist visits would disappear if certain types of action were taken. In fact, merely the election of a candidate likely to take actions offensive to the hegemonic power would normally be enough for the armed forces to intervene and nullify the elections. Although the specific line that cannot be crossed without bringing about some form of retribution shifts with different U.S. administrations, the key variables are encroachment on the property rights of U.S. citizens and companies and support for the power currently an adversary of the United States in international politics.[5] In circumstances like these, it would be misleading simply to describe the Dominican political process without noting the implicit limits, the boundary lines within which the game takes place.[6]

What is true of the hegemony of the foreign power may also apply to the hegemony of a preponderant domestic interest, a financial power center, or even a dominant socioeconomic class as a whole. What may occur, that is, is that the people making policy decisions do not need to be subjected to direct pressure or representations in specific cases; they may simply "understand the situation," that is, be aware that unfortunate consequences would be in store if certain interests are harmed, with the result that that kind of decision is simply never taken. And yet a further step is possible: Awareness may be unconscious or implicit in underlying cultural understandings, so that certain classes of options are foreclosed to the decision-maker because they are "unthinkable."

For different types of political systems and different types of society, different categories of policy options will be unthinkable. In the United States, no decision-maker would consider as options the taking of private property without compensation or the indefinite imprisonment of someone without trial; in the Soviet Union or Paraguay, these might be live options, while the indictment of a member of the political police would not.

The character of the political system conditions the decision-making process in this fundamental sense, of setting the parameters outside which certain options become unthinkable. But the structure of the political system also affects the participation in the policymaking process of interest groups and of career public servants in two significant ways. First, pressure group activity will focus at those points in the structure of public power at which decisions are effectively made, and this will vary from system to system. Thus, for example, in the United States the national legislature has power independent of the executive, and that power is diffused throughout the body, with individual committee chairmen and legislators playing significant roles. By contrast, the British House of Commons operates by party discipline, so that the impact of individual members of Parliament who are in the opposition or back-benchers (that is, who are not members of the government) is very limited. Accordingly, in the United States, a great deal of lobbying activity is directed at influencing members of Congress. It is true, as C. Wright Mills has written, that from one point of view Congress occupies only the middle levels of power, while the fundamental questions have to be taken by Congress as givens; that is, Congress operates within parameters set by the assumptions on which the system is based.[7] Nevertheless, at those middle levels of power decisions are taken that can mean prosperity or ruin for individual firms or whole industries, for example, and thus a great deal of pressure group activity focuses on the Congress. Of course, it is also directed at the executive branch, both its partisan political leadership and its permanent career levels; in Britain, interest group pressure focuses almost exclusively on the executive branch. However, in both countries efforts are also directed at the general public in the attempt to mold opinion that will then have its effect on government action. That sort of activity would be wasted effort in many countries of the world, where public opinion is in normal times of little influence on government action. Thus the pattern of power in a specific period of history in a specific country necessarily determines the pattern followed by interest group pressure.

IV

It should also be noted that different systems place differently the line that separates the permanent bureaucracy of career public servants from the echelon of partisan political leadership. In principle, permanent career officials are charged with the implementation of general policies that are set by the political leadership, who are responsible to the voters who choose them in periodic elections. Of course in practice the line is not a hard and fast one and career officials may in fact modify the policy by the way they implement it. They are in any case influential in determining what the policy will be. Equally, elected politicians may become involved in questions of administrative detail. Nevertheless, the distinction remains a significant one.

It is therefore striking how much the application of the general principle varies from one system to another. At one extreme, in Britain the political echelon is very thin, with only about 100 positions changing occupants when the opposition party comes to power after an election.[8] In some ministries only the top two or three positions change hands. Thus the career public service reaches almost to the pinnacle of the government. In such circumstances, one might expect that policies would vary very little between governments of one party and those of another, with the permanent civil servants in fact setting policy and not simply implementing it. This is indeed the argument made by Richard Rose in his book *Do Parties Make a Difference?*[9] But that seems to be the case only when the party leadership itself has no clear idea of where it is going and simply restricts itself to managing the daily crises. A committed government with a distinctive program, such as that of Prime Minister Margaret Thatcher, does indeed depart from the parameters of middle-of-the-road consensus and finds that the civil service does its bidding in any case. This was something of a surprise to some members of the Labour government of 1945–50, led by Clement Attlee; the Labour party chairman of the time, Harold Laski, had thought at one point that the civil service would refuse to implement a socialist program.

Sweden carries the separation between politics and administration to its ultimate point. In Sweden, members of the cabinet do not have control over the executive department of government, which are headed by career public servants. The departments implement the legislation that has been passed, subject to fiscal, auditing, and legal controls, while the cabinet affects policy principally by embodying its views in legislative projects submitted to parliament.

In the United States, by contrast, the election of a new president means not only the replacement of the cabinet but the replacement of subcabinet officials, bureau chiefs, and staff members. If barely 100 posts change hands in Britain, perhaps 10,000 do so in the United States. In France and Germany, yet another pattern obtains, with career civil servants who have reached a certain point in the hierarchy frequently becoming politicians and offering themselves for election. Four of the ten prime ministers who have served in the French Fifth Republic, and two of the four presidents, began their careers in the professional public service, civil or military.

In West Germany, the pattern is for civil servants to take leave from their positions in order to serve in elective public office, during which time they continue to accumulate service credit toward their pensions. This helps to give West German parliamentarism its bureaucratic flavor, as members of a specialized committee of the Bundestag, the federal assembly, may well have been colleagues in the federal ministry dealing with the committee's subject matter. The bureaucratic character of the legislature is further heightened because the upper house— the Bundesrat, or federal council, which represents the states— is normally made up of delegations of permanent officials sent by the state governments.

While in all democratic countries, accordingly, a line of demarcation exists between bureaucracy and political leadership, the line is differently placed and is of different degrees of permeability from one side or the other.

V

The most fruitful way to conceptualize the process of policymaking is thus as the province of a bureaucracy responding to (1) the concept of the public interest embodied in legislation; (2) pressure from the groups and interests most directly affected; and (3) the interests, personal and institutional, and styles of behavior of the bureaucrats themselves. Elected political officials affect the process but only intermittently, by intervening directly, by legislating, by changing the terms of public debate, and by altering the rules under which pressure groups must operate. Limiting and conditioning the behavior and objectives of bureaucrats and politicians alike are the underlying assumptions reflecting the norms of the political and economic systems.

NOTES

1. Thus in Mexico, for example, any business having declared assets over a specified amount must belong to local chambers of either commerce or industry, which are grouped into two "peak" organizations at the federal level.

2. Neil Mitchell, "Public Policy, Policy Style, and Pressure Group Influence," paper presented at the annual meeting of the Midwestern Political Science Association, April 1985.

3. Called by Anthony Birch "the Westminster model." See his *The British System of Government*, 6th ed., London: Allen and Unwin, 1983, pp. 22–26.

4. Gavin Lyall writes in *Blame the Dead*, New York: Viking, 1973, p. 36:

Civil Service air. They mix it up in a secret plant south of the river and pipe it out to all the offices all over London. You can see the pipes running along the underground tunnels next time you're in a train. It's good for you. Breathe enough of it and you lose all anger, all pity, all concern. And you never die; you only fade away like the red ink on an old forgotten file.

5. Cole Blasier, *The Hovering Giant*, Pittsburgh: University of Pittsburgh Press, 1976.

6. See Jan K. Black, *The Dominican Republic: Politics in an Unsovereign State*, Westport, Conn.: Greenwood Press, 1986.

7. C. Wright Mills, *The Power Elite*, New York: Oxford University Press, 1956.

8. However, posts outside the national government structure itself, on advisory boards and in the public sector of industry, are subject to change.

9. Richard Rose, *Do Parties Make a Difference?* 2nd U.S. ed., Chatham, N.J.: Chatham House Publishers, 1984.

11

EXECUTIVES, LEGISLATURES, AND THE SEPARATION OF POWERS

I

Almost all the democratic regimes—that is, those whose powers with respect to the citizenry are limited and whose leadership derives, directly or indirectly, from popular elections—that exist in the world today fall into two major types, presidential and parliamentary. Broadly speaking, in the parliamentary system the executive is elected by, or is otherwise responsible to, the legislature, while in the presidential system the chief executive is elected independent of the legislature.

Three types of political systems today do not fall into either the parliamentary or presidential categories, however. In one type the constitutional structure, usually of consultative councils of various kinds, is no more than a façade for a disguised dictatorship. Fascist and pseudo-corporatist regimes fall into this category, as do the novel structures erected by revolutionary military leaders in countries of Asia and the Middle East, sometimes purportedly reflecting Islamic precepts.

The second category includes systems that try to function without an individual chief executive. These "collegial" systems include some postrevolutionary regimes, such as the assembly government of the early days of the French Revolution, or the collective leadership of the first years of the Sandinista government in Nicaragua. These systems may transform themselves, as in the Nicaraguan example, into one of more traditional type; or they may retain the forms of collective leadership as a façade for a dictatorship. Collective leadership has, however, survived in the Swiss system, in which the cabinet as a whole exercises executive power and all parties participate in the cabinet. Stability under this kind of arrangement no doubt owes a great deal to the peculiar circumstances of Swiss politics, under which a great deal of power resides in the governments of the cantons rather than the government of the federation, and in which major questions are decided directly by the voters in referenda. In other words, collective leadership may survive at the federal level only because the range of issues decided at that level is relatively small. The experience of Uruguay, which copied the Swiss model, has at any rate not been encouraging. A modified version of the Swiss collegial executive, dividing powers between a collective leadership and a president, was adopted by the Uruguayans in 1917 and abolished in 1933, but then the full version, without a national president, was put into effect for the years 1954–66. Regrettably, the collegial executive proved divided and indecisive and was unable to take effective action to deal with the difficult economic circumstances in which Uruguay found itself during the period.

The third category consists of systems that have attempted to combine features of the parliamentary and presidential regimes. In this category at the time of writing are Finland, Poland, Peru, and France, and experiments of this kind have taken place in various countries over the years. Experience with hybrid forms of this kind has been mixed, as we shall see in the following chapter.

II

Although almost all of the world's countries function on the basis of a written constitution, which may give the impression that their institutions were logically designed, the origins of both parliamentary and presidential systems are to be found not in logic but in history. They have indeed the same historical origin, both being developments from the political tradition of Britain. British institutions were copied in modified form by the French, and other countries became incorporated into the French or British traditions by imitating France or Britain, or by being colonized by them.

Britain itself has no written constitution as such and British institutions have evolved over the years, so that different institutional structures have resulted from the copying of British institutions at different points in time. That is in fact how the presidential system originated. Although there were setbacks and rapid advances, the history of the evolution of British institutions can be described not inaccurately as the process of the gradual stripping away of the powers of government from the monarch and the House of Lords and their concentration in the hands of the House of Commons. U.S. political institutions, at the state as well as the federal levels, originated during a transitional era in which the monarch and the House of Lords retained a great deal of power, but the House of Commons had acquired a great deal too. Thus the situation, which the colonists took to be the normal one, was a separation and division of powers among a chief executive and two houses of a legislature. Although this was a state of affairs that had evolved historically rather than as the result of a blueprint drawn up by political theorists, this kind of system was eulogized by Montesquieu as the most desirable. Power was divided, with one institution checking another, so that it was less likely to be abused. In fact, there has never been a shortage of political theorists to eulogize the British system as they understood it to exist at any given moment of time.

Practice in Britain paid no attention to theory, however. Power continued to gravitate to the House of Commons and away from the monarch and the House of Lords, encouraged by the spread of modern ideas of rationality, equality, and democracy. The United States retained the separation of powers as it had existed in Britain during the seventeenth century, however, although eventually the suffrage for the Senate was democratized and the presidential electoral college became only a formality. The British system evolved into one resting on a fusion of powers, with all power residing in the House of Commons, while the House of Lords and the monarch were reduced, finally, to very little more than purely formal roles.

The logic of a system in which powers are fused is quite different from that of one in which they are separated. In the British-style parliamentary system, the party or coalition of parties that controls a majority of seats in the assembly forms the government and introduces the great bulk of legislative projects. If any significant legislative initiatives are defeated by the assembly, this signifies that the heretofore dominant party or coalition has lost its majority and should therefore be replaced by representatives of a new majority. In other words, there must be agreement between the cabinet and the legislative majority for the system to function. This is different from the separation-of-powers system, which assumes that a minimum of jealous hostility or at least rivalry is present between executive and legislature, so that each will act to prevent any abuse of power by the other.

III

Conventionally, therefore, it is said that parliamentary systems embody a fusion of powers, and presidential systems embody a separation of powers. The separation of powers is inevitably represented as a separation among three branches of government: executive, legislative, and judicial. The three branches are described as making the laws, enforcing the laws, and interpreting the laws, respectively. Following Montesquieu and Madison, the reason given for this arrangement is that it safeguards liberty; the freedom of the subject would be at risk if the same agency were both to make the laws and to enforce them, or to enforce them and adjudicate them. Americans accept this doctrine rather as though it were religious dogma; as though there were tablets of stone laid up in heaven engraved with the separation of powers into the three branches. Many of my students have difficulty accepting the possibility that a parliamentary system that does not feature the conventional separation of powers can in fact be called democratic.

There are, however, several major difficulties with the separation of powers doctrine as it is generally understood and as it is embodied in constitutional arrangements in the United States. First, is the division into only three "powers" satisfactory? Several Latin American and Asian constitutions, for example, have recognized a separate "electoral power," an autonomous system of tribunals that organizes and conducts elections, on the premise that it would invite abuses of power if elections were organized and conducted by officials who themselves are chosen by the same electoral process. Voters in many U.S. jurisdictions will no doubt recognize the merit of the argument.

The Chinese Nationalist Constitution of Dr. Sun Yat-Sen also recognized a separate "control power," a body having especially auditing functions. These functions are lodged in the United States in the General Accounting Office, a dependency of Congress, and to some extent in the Internal Revenue Service (IRS) and the Federal Bureau of Investigation (FBI), within the executive branch. As might be expected, the IRS and the FBI have on occasion been used to serve the personal and partisan objectives of the politician who serves as president; the General Accounting Office has a good reputation as an impartial investigator, although it is only intermittently called upon. Both Chile and Costa Rica have an independent office of comptroller-general with autonomous auditing powers, which can investigate individuals holding office in any of the branches of government. The Scandinavian ombudsman serves as an autonomous investigator, especially of administrative acts, on behalf of individual citizens. The general point to be made is that there are important ways of protecting the liberties of the citizen, involving investigative, monitoring, and auditing functions, which are ignored, obscured, or underemphasized by the conventional tripartite conceptualization of the separation of powers.

The second, and more obvious, question to be raised about the tripartite separation of powers is that the "executive power," as this is conventionally understood, is certainly not adequately described as simply the power concerned with executing the laws. As embodied in the U.S. executive, certainly, the "executive power" is actually a general leadership and gov-

erning power. The supervision of the implementation of laws
is only one, and not the major one, of a president's functions.
It is as though the Congress and the judiciary enjoy some powers that they have been able to subtract from the plenitude of
political power, but the vast residue, executive, legislative, and
judicial, remains with the presidency. In fact, such a process
of subtraction is not an inaccurate description of the way in
which the executive power came to be defined, as British government evolved from a situation of monarchic near-absolutism
and, over the centuries, one power after another was wrested
away from the monarch. The definition of the executive power
is more historical than logical.

Thus in foreign policy, for example, the president legislates
and implements policy as he goes along, even exercising some
judicial powers with respect to the extradition of suspects in-
dicted in other countries, or with respect to aliens seeking asy-
lum in the United States. A major function of the presidency
is to serve, in fact, as a third chamber of the legislature. With
the veto power, the president must vote on legislation, just as
the House and Senate must, for it to become law. Moreover,
he takes the lead in proposing and drafting a substantial proportion of the bills introduced. That the primary role of the
"executive power" is really legislative is formally recognized
in Sweden, where the cabinet does not have actual supervision
of the bureaucracy; the pretense that the "executive power"
has as its primary function the execution of the laws is aban-
doned. The Swedish cabinet has the role of deciding on policy
and introducing legislation to implement it in the Riksdag; the
bureaucracy runs itself, under the leadership of the highest-
ranking civil servants, who remain responsible at law for their
performance of their duties.

IV

It seems hardly exaggerated to say that in the general pan-
orama of democratic societies today, what have been called here
the auditing and control functions are not performed with the
appropriate vigor, or performed at all, so that abuses of power
by governments are quite common. Thus the first objective of

any institutional reform should be the devising of mechanisms and the structuring of incentives so that the auditing functions are not neutralized by political influences, bartered away for reasons of career advancement, or allowed to wither because of bureaucratic inertia.

The second great need of contemporary western democracies in this respect is the restoration to legislatures of powers they have lost to executive branches. Any attempt to strengthen legislatures, however, must confront a series of baffling paradoxes.

One of these paradoxes reflects a general principle of politics: If A is established in order to control B, then B will in fact control A. The controllee controls the controller. Those of us who live in states in which a public service commission is supposed to regulate the prices charged by a monopoly energy provider will understand what I mean. Because the commission regulates electricity rates, the electricity company spends a lot of money in the gray area of political finance, in campaign contributions, consultation fees, and the hiring of politicians and their relatives to acquire the influence necessary to determine that the appointees to the public service commission will reflect its interests.

Similarly, in a parliamentary system in which the legislature may remove the cabinet by a vote of confidence, the cabinet develops mechanisms to control the way the legislature votes. The party leadership develops the norm of party discipline and reinforces it with punitive sanctions. In the British House of Commons, for example, in the twentieth century a cabinet has never been overthrown by a vote of no confidence as a result of defections from the majority party (although cabinets have left office for other reasons). To the extent that a legislature performs as an electoral college, accordingly, its powers will tend to be assumed by the majority party leadership.

In this case the exception proves the rule, as it were. In a separation-of-powers system, such as that of the United States, the head of government is elected separately from the legislature, so that if the legislature votes against his policies it does not threaten his remaining in office, as it would in a parliamentary system. A president serves to the end of his fixed term; he does not resign if he loses a vote in Congress. However, there is one type of vote in which the houses of Congress do act as an electoral college, and it is precisely in that vote, and only in that vote, that party discipline holds and the members simply vote with their party leadership. This is the vote to organize the house, that is, to decide which party controls the committee chairmanships and, in the House of Representatives, elects the Speaker. So long as the fate of the government depends on its vote, accordingly, a legislature can be expected to consist, in the picturesque phrase used in German parliamentarism, of "voting cattle," whipped into the division lobbies by the party leadership.

Yet in separation-of-powers systems in which the house is not subject to party discipline of this type because it does not serve as an electoral college, a further paradox is presented. Given the necessity of checking the executive branch, that is, of performing oversight with respect to the bureaucracy and imposing responsibility for their acts on cabinet members, the legislature needs to develop expertise in specific areas of policy. This requires specialization, such as is achieved in the U.S. Congress by the committee system. A capable and long-serving committee chairman can be a match for a cabinet minister who may not have been long in his job, despite the fact that the latter can call on the expertise of his staff. The chairman and his committee are then in a position of being able to recommend to the full house changes in the legislation governing the operations and policies of the department in question, and the house normally defers to the judgment of the specialized committee and especially of its chairman. Because of the expectation that this will be the case, the chairman is able to influence actions of the bureaucracy. But what are we saying here? The legislature has power, but only in so far as that power is wielded in effect by a specific individual or limited group of individuals. Yet because of the lack of party discipline and of a coherent party position on issues, the views of the chairman may not in fact reflect the views that a majority of the members of the legislative body might have if they were sufficiently informed about the issue in question. The committee chairman is in this case an individual politician answering to a specific constituency which may itself not be representative of the country as a whole, not to mention the obligations he may have to specific interest groups.

Ironically, even where a legislature has power, it is not the legislature as a whole that has the power. Much of the power of the legislature is wielded either by the majority party leadership or by the committee chairmen.

12

THE PARLIAMENTARY-
PRESIDENTIAL HYBRID

I

The two most important cases in which the attempt was made to combine presidential and parliamentary regimes were those of the First German Republic (the Weimar Republic, 1919–33) and the French Fifth Republic, 1958 to the present. The reasons for the adoption of the combined presidential-parliamentary system in those countries, which rested partly on a misunderstanding of the way parliamentary systems necessarily operate, provide an extraordinary chapter in the history of ideas.

The constitution of the German Republic was adopted by a constituent assembly that met at Weimar in 1919. The right-wing parties, the Conservatives and the National Liberals, favored a presidential system with a strong president, if the monarchy could not be continued. The left-wing parties, the larger of which, the Social Democrats, was in the government of the time, favored a strong parliament with at most a weak figure-head president to be elected by the parliament itself. The balance of power in the constituent assembly was held by the other two parties of the governing coalition, the Catholic Center

Party and the liberals of the German Democratic Party. These
two parties were, however, under contradictory pressures on
the question. They had both fought for years, under the imperial system that collapsed with the defeat of World War I,
to establish the principle of cabinet responsibility to the legislature, and had become committed to it. However, there was
a great deal of support within the two parties for a strong,
popularly elected president. This derived in part from the pop-
ularity of Woodrow Wilson, whose proposals for a peace treaty,
the so-called Fourteen Points, were welcomed as saving Germany from humiliation. The strong, popularly elected presidency was also being urged by prominent liberal theorists,
especially Max Weber, who regarded it as necessary in order
to establish some sort of democratic control over Germany's
traditionally powerful bureaucracy.

The question was resolved by Hugh Preuss, the professor of
constitutional law who served as minister of the interior in the
provisional government. His solution was based on a new interpretation of parliamentary government that had been published the previous year, written by an Alsatian professor of
constitutional law, Robert Redslob.[1] Redslob's interpretation
of parliamentarism was based on his study of parliamentary
politics in England in the eighteenth century, which had led
him to the view that the essence of genuine parliamentarism
was that it depended on a balance of power between executive
and legislature. Cabinet and parliament checked each other,
in this version; if the cabinet abused its powers, it could be
removed by the legislature, while an intractable parliament
could be dissolved by the prime minister and new elections
called. Now this interpretation is misleading since, to the extent that a balance of power exists in the British Parliament,
it is not between executive and legislature, but between majority and opposition. The opposition checks the government,
and the parliamentary majority that supports it, through its
questions and its role in debates. The checks to the abuse of
power lie in party competition, informing the electorate, and
influencing the outcome of the next election, and not in a myth-
ical distribution of powers between "executive" and "legislature." The power of dissolution is sometimes said to be a

constraint on the backbenchers of the majority party, who are deterred from deserting the party in voting because the party's loss of its majority may bring about new elections and a chance of losing their seats in the House. This, again, is rather far-fetched and of only incidental, if any, significance. Backbenchers of the majority party support the government because they believe in it, because they are loyal, because they were elected principally for their party affiliation and not for their individual merits, because no matter how much they dissent they prefer their own party's program to that of the opposition, and because the reward of eventual cabinet membership is more likely to come to the loyal than to the dissident.

Having made the power to dissolve parliament so central to his analysis, however, Redslob then compounded his error by misunderstanding why the dissolution of parliament was not used in the contemporary French Third Republic while it was used in Britain. Redslob argued that although the French president legally had the power to dissolve the assembly, in fact he never exercised the power because he was no more than the creature of the assembly; it elected him, so he had no independent will or source of legitimacy. The British prime minister, however, did exercise his power to dissolve Parliament, Redslob thought, because he had such an independent position and source of legitimacy by virtue of his appointment by the monarch.

This is really a dreadful misunderstanding, which reflects eighteenth-century and not twentieth-century reality, to the extent that it is accurate at all. Appointment by the monarch is today a formality without practical significance; the prime ministers in a democratic era owe their positions to their leadership of the majority party in Parliament. The French president in the Third Republic may indeed not have dissolved the parliament because he had no independent role; nevertheless, he could have dissolved at the request of the prime minister, just as it is the British monarch who formally dissolves the House of Commons on the request of the prime minister. French prime ministers did not ask for dissolutions of the parliament for two main reasons. First, dissolution had a bad name in France because it had been used by an early president of the

Third Republic, Marshal MacMahon, apparently as prelude to an attempted coup d'état. Second, and more importantly, cabinets in the Third Republic were multi-party coalitions. They were re-formed frequently, with parties joining or dropping out depending on the issues to be confronted. In the predominantly two-party British system, if a government lost its majority because some of its supporters deserted to the opposition, dissolution and new elections would establish which camp had a majority and could support a government. In a multi-party system, however, a dissolution and new elections would not give a clear majority to one side or the other. Why resort to a remedy that was no remedy at all?

But because dissolution was a necessary part of parliamentarism in the Redslob scheme, and because a French-style president, elected by the assembly, did not have the independent authority to dissolve the assembly—even though he may have had the legal right to do it—how was "genuine" parliamentarism to be instituted in a country, like Germany, whose monarch had abdicated? Preuss resolved the problem in the only way that seemed logically possible, but which at the same time incorporated the desire among liberals and centrists for a strong, popularly elected president. Such a president, unlike the weak one of the French Third Republic, would have the authority independent of the legislature that would enable him to authorize its dissolution, thus making genuine parliamentarism possible. In this view, therefore, the strong, popularly elected president was not an alternative to the parliamentary system, which one might think in view of the U.S. model, but was in fact necessary to the working of parliamentarism in a non-monarchic system.

Now in fact this model misinterprets the functioning of the parliamentary system, in both its logic and its evolution. This resulted, in the hybrid system that was created at Weimar, in a difficulty and a danger. The difficulty lies in control of the cabinet. The prime minister ("chancellor" in the German system) and cabinet are designated by the president. At the same time they are removable by a vote of no confidence by the assembly. They must, in other words, serve two masters. There would be no difficulty if the president were content to remain little more than a figurehead and appoint whomever would get a majority in the parliament. There would equally be no problem, on the other hand, if the cabinet were not responsible to the legislature, as in the U.S. system, and remained in office even if the legislature refused to pass any of the legislation the president or the cabinet proposed. In the hybrid system, however, a strong, popularly elected president naturally attempts to direct the policy of the government, which he logically does through his designation of the cabinet and his guidance of their policies. No problem exists if the president and the legislative majority are of the same party. Since they are elected in a different manner and at different times, however, sooner or later it can be expected that the legislative majority will be of a political tendency opposed to that of the president, at which point the control of the cabinet and of government policy becomes a bone of contention. At such a time the danger exists either that stalemate and chaos set in, as the assembly persistently votes to remove cabinets and the president obstinately persists in appointing cabinets to carry out the same policies; or alternatively that the president insists on having his way, maintains his cabinet in office despite legislative disapproval, and legislates through decree powers. In fact, the latter is what happened in the Weimar Republic. The constitution provided for presidential rule by decree powers under a state of emergency which the president himself could proclaim, and the period that preceded Hitler's appointment as chancellor was one of presidential dictatorship under emergency powers.

The Basic Law of the Second German Republic, the regime under which West Germany is currently ruled, is carefully designed so that that set of circumstances cannot be reproduced. The president is elected by an electoral college, not by direct popular vote. His choice to be chancellor must be confirmed by a majority legislative vote and can only be removed by another majority legislative vote, and an emergency can only be declared with the concurrence of both president and chancellor. Even then, emergency legislation must still be approved by the upper house of the federal legislature.

II

Curiously enough, the hybrid presidential-parliamentary system adopted by the French Fifth Republic in 1958 had the same intellectual origin as the Weimar system. The University of Strasbourg, where Redslob held his chair of constitutional law, was in the province of Alsace, which had been taken from France and annexed to Germany in 1870 and remained German until the end of World War I. Thus Professor Redslob wrote in German and was able to influence the writing of the Weimar constitution, even being quoted by members of the committee that drew up the constitution. However, in 1919 Alsace rejoined France. Eventually Redslob himself passed on, but the distinctive Strasbourg tradition in constitutional theory was maintained by Redslob's younger colleague Raymond Carré de Malberg. One of Carré de Malberg's students, Michel Debré, went on to be an aide to General de Gaulle, chief author of the constitution of the Fifth French Republic, and de Gaulle's first prime minister under its terms.[2]

Extraordinarily enough, the doctrine again fitted the circumstances. The Fourth Republic had collapsed over the Algerian crisis and de Gaulle seemed the only person whose coming to power could forestall civil war. Yet he would return to power only on condition that he be allowed to propose to the voters a new constitution which would embody a strong presidency, unlike the constitution of the Fourth Republic, whose adoption had caused his resignation as head of government in 1946. Such a president, in de Gaulle's view, would have to wield considerable emergency powers to be prepared to deal with situations like the current Algerian crisis, or like the one that had constituted the crisis of the formative period of de Gaulle's first involvement in politics—the collapse of the Third Republic at the time of the German invasion in 1940.

At the same time, the parliamentarians who voted power to de Gaulle in 1958 stipulated the condition that the new constitution would have to retain parliamentary responsibility of the cabinet. This derived from the fear of a strong presidency traditional to French democrats, which grew out of the experience of the Second Republic (1848–52). At that time the voters had elected as president Louis Napoléon Bonaparte, who had proceeded to stage a coup d'état and proclaim himself emperor as Napoleon III.

The situation thus resembled that of Germany in 1919. Politically, the optimal solution seemed to be to combine presidential and parliamentary systems, and again a constitutional theorist under the influence of the Strasbourg School was the principal drafter of the constitutional document. Again it was believed that parliamentary responsibility of the cabinet could be combined with a strong, popularly elected president; and again that formula guaranteed that a crisis would arise when a legislative majority was elected opposed to the political tendency of the president.

That day did not arrive, in the case of the Fifth Republic, for 27 years, during which time first three presidents represented a coalition of Gaullists and conservatives, as did the legislative majority, after which a Socialist president enjoyed a Socialist majority in the assembly.

Finally, however, in 1986 the day arrived when a president who still had two years to complete in his term of office was confronted by a legislature in which the coalition supporting him was in the minority. Logically, there would seem to be three possibilities. First, the situation could lead to stalemate and deadlock, with the assembly majority refusing to accept the prime minister and cabinet designated by the president, and the president vetoing any legislation passed by the assembly. Second, the president could insist on having his way, resorting to his emergency powers under the constitution to create a quasi-legal dictatorship. Third, the president could designate a prime minister and cabinet representative of the new legislative majority and confine himself to a ceremonial role, or even resign. The Socialist president who found himself in this situation, François Mitterrand, had been a committed democrat all of his life, so that the second alternative, that of presidential dictatorship, was unthinkable. In any event, the state institutions through which a dictatorship would have to be conducted—the bureaucracy, the judiciary, the police, and especially the armed forces—tend to be politically conservative and would likely be unwilling instruments of a Socialist-led dictatorship. In the Weimar Republic, by contrast, these institutions had shown little reluctance to being used as organs of a right-wing dictatorship.

Mitterrand chose a variant of the third option, which the French termed "cohabitation," appointing a conservative prime minister but reserving to himself veto powers in the event he believed some government action to be unconstitutional or against the fundamental national interests. In taking this position, Mitterrand had in mind the judgment of the voters at the next presidential election, who were thought to be unlikely to accept politically motivated attempts to create deadlock and obstruct government business, but would look favorably on the assumption of a lofty position marked by dignity and patriotism. What the period of cohabitation seems to show is that although under unfavorable circumstances the mixed presidential-parliamentary system leads to stalemate or dictatorship, under favorable conditions it can function either as a presidential system or as a parliamentary one.

III

Thus, in Peru, for example, the mixed system results in practice in a presidential system with some minor parliamentary features; Cuba had a similar system prior to the revolution of 1959. In Finland, the government operates rather as it did in France under cohabitation, as a parliamentary system in which the president serves to guarantee fidelity to constitutional norms and to a particular foreign policy orientation.

Finland has the special circumstance of being the neighbor of the Soviet Union, which, after meeting fierce resistance to its 1940 attempt to subjugate and annex the country, settled for an independent state whose foreign policy would not be anti-Soviet. A president independent of the legislature, given authority over the country's foreign policy and insulated from the eventualities of the country's parliamentary politics, thus provided a guarantee acceptable to the Soviet Union.

This model was extended to Poland in 1989, when the Soviet Union accepted the first non-Communist prime minister and cabinet in 40 years. The Communist party leader, General

Wojcek Jaruzelski, was reelected president by the votes of the non-Communist Solidarity movement in order to provide the Russians with a guarantee that their minimum security needs would be safeguarded, no matter what else would change. In this way the hybrid presidential-parliamentary system, which represents a retreat from sound constitutional-democratic practices for a country that has been a functioning democracy, may constitute a movement toward democracy for a country emerging from dictatorship. Similarly, Portugal adopted the hybrid system in the constitution of 1976, the president serving to guarantee to the military that their interests would be protected. However, the constitution was amended to create a purely parliamentary system with a figurehead president when full democracy could be attained in 1988.

NOTES

1. Robert Redslob, *Die Parliamentarische Regierung in Ihrer Wahren und Unechten Form*, Tuebingen: Mohr, 1918.
2. Nicholas Wahl, "The French Constitution of 1958: The Initial Draft and its Origins," *American Political Science Review*, June 1959, p. 378; Michael Debré, "The Constitution of 1958, Its Raison d'Etre and How It Evolved," in William G. Andrews and Stanley Hoffman, eds., *The Impact of the Fifth Republic of France*, Albany: State University of New York Press, 1981.

V

CONCLUSION

13

IDENTITY, INTEREST, IDEOLOGY

In a recent article Gabriel Almond has emphasized the fragmented nature of political science, classifying the diverging methodological approaches and political predilections of its practitioners.[1] In fact, we do work with discrete bodies of subject matter that hardly appear related to each other, and at different levels of analysis. One commonly begins a description of political science to an outsider with the comment, "Well, political science is not really a single integrated discipline." My present purpose is to suggest a way in which this fragmentation can be reduced and the discipline can become conceptually more integrated.[2]

I

Public choice theory, as Professor Almond reminds us, adopts the economist's "hard-nosed" approach, postulating the thesis that an individual's vote, for example, reflects only her own selfish material interest. I think it is both misleading and unproductive to criticize this approach, as is normally done, on the grounds that it omits consideration of altruistic and public-interest-regarding behavior. The separation into "realist" and "idealist" schools of analysis that this dichotomization of perspectives engenders can instead be transcended by a different approach to the problem. Let us start with a critique of the vote as a self-interested act.

If an individual did indeed rationally consult only her immediate personal interest on election day, she would in fact not go to the effort and expense of voting, since the chance that her vote will affect the outcome is infinitesimal.[3] In fact, because of this negligible likelihood of actual effect, the vote should probably be regarded primarily as an expressive, rather than an instrumental, act. The mere holding of specific political opinions, similarly, by itself has no effect. Nevertheless, it seems fair to argue that both the vote and the opinions can in general be expected to reflect the views of the person involved as to where both the public interest and her own self-interest (in some combination) lie. Of course, the actual relation of the voting outcome to the immediate interest of the specific individual may not be manifest, so that the voter relies on surrogates of various kinds. She votes for the candidate of her party, or of her ethnic group, or of her part of town, on the probability that self-interest will be served by voting for someone belonging to one or another of the sets of people with whom she identifies. Is she still voting in her own self-interest? Apparently so. We are accustomed to use "self" in an extended sense, after all; an individual may be said to be acting out of self-interest, as opposed to acting altruistically, when she acts in the interest of her family, company, or social class. What does this imply?

A human infant is a particularly helpless creature. The species has only survived because parents—often at some personal sacrifice, sometimes even at the sacrifice of their lives—have taken the time and trouble to nurture it. The species, that is, has survived because the individual has developed a capacity for defending the interests of some other creatures as much as he does his own. There is an instinct, it is often said, for self-defense. Parents extend this instinct for self-defense to their helpless young. Since some readers may feel uncomfortable with this use of the word "self," preferring to limit it to the biological individual, let us instead use the term "identity" and say that parents identify themselves for purposes of defense and nurturance not only as individuals but also as members of families.

This capability of extending the conceptualization of one's identity, even though its evolutionary purpose may have been to develop the family feeling necessary to nurture infants, is regularly harnessed to the service of social formations beyond the family. Under various circumstances when I need to ascribe to myself an identity, because sides are being picked up and interests contested, it becomes relevant that I work for the ABC company, live in XYZ country, or speak the L language. I may then act in some sense in my "own" interest when I act on behalf of one of these collectivities with which I identify, even though perhaps at some cost to the interests of my immediate physical identity.

Acting out of interest is conventionally contrasted with altruism, or acting on behalf of others. But what does this mean, if some actions taken out of "self"-interest are in fact actions on behalf of others—members of my family or my social class, for example—anyway? If I give charity to the needy, or act chivalrously to an enemy on the battlefield, I may do so because I recognize our common humanity—that is, I am acknowledging our common identity as members of the human race. Why should that be a less salient or vivid identity to me than my identity as a member of a different social class or national community from the person I am aiding? The answer is: It may not be. In fact, different individuals give quite different weights to their different identities. Bill is primarily a family man and a Methodist of Welsh descent. Bob is above all a Texan, a Dallas Cowboys fan, and an American; whereas Walter is a Virginian, proud of his aristocratic English lineage, and nostalgic for the lost cause, who regards the Stars and Stripes with indifference. Mary identifies with women and near-sighted people the world over. These differing identities structure these people's political opinions and behavior. Once we accept that the "self" in self-interest does not necessarily refer only to the single biological individual but extends to the sets with which the individual identifies, it becomes difficult to maintain the conceptual distinction between self-interested and altruistic behavior.

Let us suppose, then, that we can transcend the distinction between the pursuit of interest and altruism by stipulating that all intentional political acts involve the pursuit of the interests of the collectivities with which individuals identify, which can extend to a set as large as the whole species (or to all sentient creation, for that matter) or one limited to one or a few individuals.

Now of course the nation-state, by contriving a near-monopoly of force and proselytizing for the doctrine of sovereignty, has managed to work itself into a preeminent place among those collectivities in whose interests we strive. Through the symbolism of flags and anthems, by achieving a dominant position in education, by attaching fearsome penalties to disloyalty to itself, the nation-state has largely succeeding in getting itself accepted as the preeminent political community, the supreme source of identity, and thus the owner and operator of the ultimate interests that are to be served. It is long past time that these pretensions were scaled down to size. My own view is that the most compelling loyalties are to the smallest and the largest collectivities, the family and the species; the claims of the intermediate ones seem more arbitrary and not as obviously justifiable.

There is no need to take a position on that question, however, for our present purposes.

II

So far, we can see that political science studies the behavior of individuals, singly or collectively, as they pursue the interests of the sets of people with whom they identify. The appreciation that these identifications are multiple is extremely important, making it possible to understand or "retrodict" behavior as rationally maximizing to a greater extent than it would otherwise be. Actions that seem irrational or explicable only on the basis of mysterious "cultural" or "emotional" predilections when a single, apparently appropriate, identification is assumed can be seen to be perfectly rational on the basis of another, perhaps *a priori* less obvious or less appropriate, identification. A Western economist might regard a Third World

entrepreneur as not acting rationally to maximize his income
because of his lack of efficiency in labor utilization, when in
fact he was acting rationally to maximize the income of his
extended family by ensuring that all of his otherwise unem-
ployable relations were employed.

This appreciation that identifications are multiple has often
been the basis for sensational advances and breakthroughs in
the social sciences, when it is intermittently rediscovered in
specific contexts. Thus Graham Allison scored a significant success when he pointed out, among other things, that decision-
makers in the Cuban military crisis were not only representatives of national governments but also members of bureau-
cracies. Anthony Leeds, William Mangin, and others turned
around our understanding of Third World shantytown populations by suggesting that they acted not merely as members
of a social class but also, where appropriate, as heads of families. That is, they were not politically revolutionary, as class
analysis suggested they should be, so much as politically con-
tented in that urban residence improved the life chances of
their children. I myself have made a fair-to-middling living out
of revealing that Latin American military officers act not simply as public-spirited servants of the state but also out of their
own caste interests. Brilliant careers are still to be constructed
on the basis of the rediscovery and application of this principle,
perhaps especially in the fields of voting behavior and international relations.

There is thus no reason that the study of these fields, or that
of parties and pressure groups, of legislatures and bureaucra-
cies—indeed, of everything political science can study—should
not be much more homologous than it is. In principle, opinions
expressed or actions taken, whether by voters, bureaucrats, or
foreign ministers, can equally well be interpreted in terms of
the rational pursuit of the interests of the collectivities with
which individuals identify. After the analysis of enough ex-
perimental data, it may even be possible to assign relative
weights and frequencies to different possible identifications.

In the study of the Latin American military, for instance, it
has been possible to do this, albeit so far in rather gross terms.[4]
In a military seizure of power, for example, a variety of indi-

vidual patterns of self-identification is always present, some officers being particularly concerned about social class interests, others about their branch of service, and so on. This makes the conspiracy to seize power a coalition of people with differing structures of motivation, which exhibits characteristic patterns of coalition behavior. The strongest motivating factors are the collective interests of military officers and the institutional interests of the armed forces, which all participants share. These usually, but not always, mandate the same behavior as the class interests of the dominant social class or the interests of the hegemonic power (currently the United States) but, in the event of conflict, military interests take precedence.[5]

All of these sets of interests come into play through the medium of individual behavior. An individual may act solely as a representative of the interests of a single collectivity; however, this is less likely than that he represent more than one. Even the U.S. ambassador, and certainly the U.S. military attaché, has to establish priorities among his own self-identifications before he acts or gives advice.

III

In fact, individuals do not choose and weight their various self-identifications anew each time political action is called for. Individuals, such as the voter with whom we started, generally evolve over time, and then maintain moderately constant over time a sense of how their various social identities, in their relative importance, configure, and of how the constellation of interests implied by the resultant configuration relates, in general, to political issues, and indeed to general philosophical questions. The result of this process is what is called an ideology.

Not all individuals have fully elaborated and well-functioning ideologies. The pollsters tell us, in effect, that some individuals lack ideological structures completely. Moreover, different individuals' ideologies are elaborated to different degrees, and perform their function more or less well. That function is to serve as a guide when political action needs to be taken or political opinion expressed, in general or in relation to a specific question, by providing a more or less coherent account, consistent with the general interests of the collectivities with which the individual most identifies, of how the political world works and what policies are desirable.

To conceive of ideology solely as a rationalization of social class interest in Marxist fashion is thus too narrow, but correctly grasps the kind of entity ideology is, in the sense that a generalized version of personal economic interests is more or less equivalent to a statement of class interests. To compute where one's self-interest actually lies at any given moment in relation to a variety of issues, some of them quite remote from any apparent personal relevance, is asking too much. However, one can have an idea of where one's various interests lie in normal circumstances, and generalize from that to an idea of what policies are in general desirable, and to a model of how the world functions which makes plausible that those policies will work in the general public interest.

A great deal of reasoning by analogy, and of retrospective justification of one's curriculum vitae, may be involved in the formation of an ideology, which even then may provide only an approximation to a political opinion. But standards of acceptability for personal ideologies seem not to be very rigorous. Someone decides that, in general, he benefits less from government social programs than he is hurt by paying the taxes that finance them. He justifies his position, if called on to do so, by arguing that bureaucrats only waste money; that government spending programs only create dependency; that the poor and disadvantaged in whose interest those programs are supposedly designed are only lazy; that *he* was always able to find work when he wanted to; that his financial position shows that it is possible to succeed without government handouts, and so on.

That is, an ideology contains policy prescriptions, and assertions about cause-and-effect relations consistent with them, which may extend to fairly complex philosophical statements about the nature of the world. The network of reasoning the ideology contains becomes more elaborate the greater the number of different identities that are important to the individual, which the ideology must accommodate, and the greater the genuine data he has about the actual functioning of the world, which limit the factual simplications he can make. The ideological structure of a sophisticated individual of wide and unusual sympathies can thus be a very complex and impressive piece of work.

For any given individual, alternative ideologies may connect up the points on her cognitive and self-identification maps equally effectively. The choice among possible alternatives is then determined by the relative balance of emotional satisfactions, in the sense of the "externalization" of psychic dynamics, for example, that each is able to afford. Expressive functions, emotional satisfactions, psychological and cultural predispositions, certainly enter into the formation of ideologies, and into political behavior generally. The best hope for a scientific political science based on a common body of theory, however, is to expand to the maximum the scope of the behavior that can be accounted for as rational and instrumental, and thus susceptible of logical analysis.

IV

Of course, political scientists are interested in differing bodies of subject matter. Is it necessarily the case that we must also remain separated by our methodological predilections, even if it were possible to bring our subfields closer together conceptually? No, not necessarily. Different skills, different techniques, imply cooperation as much as lack of interaction. One passes, another runs, a third blocks; they are not only playing the same game, they are serving on the same team. Your tools are questionnaires, his computers and programs, mine a pad and a ballpoint pen; but we need each other in order to function.

Most of the time, for example, I work by trying to develop new theoretical formulations that comprehend disparate research findings, only a few of them my own, and generally proceed by building on the work of others, critiquing and modifying their conclusions. This seems to me a very necessary role, given the nature of scientific knowledge as a collective enterprise; it is this role I have attempted to play in writing this book.

NOTES

1. Gabriel A. Almond, "Separate Tables: Schools and Sects in Political Science," *PS* 21(4), Fall 1988.

2. Curiously enough, I can take my lesson from the same text as Professor Almond—Terence Rattigan's play *Separate Tables*. The setting in which the action takes place is indeed one of loneliness and estrangement, but the play's message, made especially clear in the climax to the second act, is that this can be transcended by human solidarity. The forces making for integration, let us say, triumph over those making for separation.

3. Rather less, as was pointed out by B. F. Skinner, than that she will be killed in a traffic accident on the way to the polling station. Quoted in W. Phillips Shively, *Power and Choice*, New York: Random House, 1987, p. 149.

4. What follows is not only much simplified, but applies in particular to the middle of the twentieth century, that is, the period since the professionalization of Latin American armies. Institutional interests were much weaker vis-à-vis class and other interests prior to that time.

5. Velasco Alvarado in Peru, Torrijos in Panama, and Perón in Argentina would be the most salient cases in living memory of military rulers who pursued policies opposed by the United States.

BIBLIOGRAPHY

Almond, Gabriel, and G. Bingham Powell. *Comparative Politics: A Developmental Approach*, 2nd ed. Boston: Little, Brown, 1978. Extensive analysis from a structural-functional perspective.

Almond, Gabriel, and Sidney Verba. *The Civic Culture*. Boston: Little, Brown, 1965. Pathbreaking though flawed exploration of the concept of political culture, particularly as it characterizes countries at different stages of development.

Aristotle. *Politics*. (Various editions). Still a great compendium of analysis and insight. Frequently a modern political scientist applies sophisticated techniques to mountains of data and ends up repeating what Aristotle said 2,000 years ago.

Black, Cyril E. *The Dynamics of Modernization*. New York: Harper & Row, 1966. An original depiction of the process of modernization in its particular historical context, rather than as a timeless or abstract process.

Blasier, Cole. *The Hovering Giant*. Pittsburgh: University of Pittsburgh Press, 1976. A careful identification of the key factors that determine U.S. policy toward revolutionary regimes in Latin America.

Bracher, Karl Dietrich. *The German Dictatorship*. New York: Praeger, 1971. Especially worthwhile for its account of the collapse of the Weimar regime.

Brinton, Crane. *Anatomy of Revolution*. Englewood Cliffs, N.J.: Prentice-Hall, 1952. Develops a model based on the common features of the English (Puritan), American, French, and Russian revolutions.

Butler, David E., and Donald Stokes. *Political Change in Britain*, 2nd ed. New York: St. Martin's Press, 1976. A masterful interpretation of partisan choice in British politics.

Conradt, David. *The German Polity*, 4th ed. New York: Longman, 1989. Good one-volume survey of German politics.

Crewe, Ivor. "How to Win a Landslide Without Really Trying: Why the Conservatives Won in 1983." In Howard Penniman and Austin Ranney, eds., *Britain at the Polls, 1983*. Washington: American Enterprise Institute, 1986. Crewe has established himself as Britain's leading elections analyst.

Davies, James C. "Toward a Theory of Revolution." *American Sociological Review*, February 1962. Seminal work arguing that revolution grows not out of oppression pure and simple, but from the frustration of rising expectations.

Deutsch, Karl W. "Social Mobilization and Political Development." *American Political Science Review*, September 1961. A fundamental contribution to the theory of political development.

Dogan, Mattei, and Dominique Pelassy. *How to Compare Nations*. 2d. ed. Chatham, N.J.: Chatham House, 1990. Survey of a great deal of comparative work, with a methodological emphasis.

Domínguez, Jorge I. *Cuba: Order and Revolution*. Cambridge, Mass.: Harvard University Press, 1978. An extensive and balanced treatment.

Downs, Anthony. *An Economic Theory of Democracy*. New York: Harper & Row, 1957. A logical model of voting and party competition in democracies.

Finer, Samuel E. *The Man on Horseback*, 2nd ed. New York: Praeger, 1971. Pioneering survey of the whys and wherefores of military intervention in politics.

Foustel de Coulanges, Numa Denis. *The Ancient City*, tr. Willard Small. New York: Doubleday Anchor, 1955 (originally published 1864). A classic interpretation of the origins of the state in ancient times.

Friedrich, Carl J. *Constitutional Government and Democracy*, rev. ed., Boston: Ginn, 1950 (first published by Harper, 1937). Eclectic and encyclopaedic, a masterpiece of the classic tradition in comparative politics.

Friedrich, Carl J., and Zbigniew Brzezinski. *Totalitarian Government and Autocracy*. Cambridge, Mass.: Harvard University Press, 1956. The most frequently cited work on totalitarianism.

Huntington, Samuel P. *Political Order in Changing Societies*. New Haven: Yale University Press, 1968. Probably the most highly regarded work on political development, complex and subtle.

Jaguaribe, Hélio. *Political Development: A General Theory and A Latin American Case Study*. New York: Harper & Row, 1973. An original and sophisticated treatment by a brilliant political scientist normally locked in the prison of the Portuguese language.

Kirkpatrick, Jeane. "Dictatorships and Double Standards," *Commentary*, November 1979. A clever but unpersuasive attempt to convert the distinction between totalitarianism and authoritarianism into one between left and right.

Lipset, Seymour Martin. *Political Man: The Social Bases of Politics*. New York: Doubleday Anchor, 1963. Provocative and wide-ranging work that pioneered the field of political development.

Markovitz, Irving Leonard. *Power and Class in Africa*. Englewood Cliffs, N.J.: Prentice-Hall, 1977. One of the better books in a generally disappointing literature.

Needler, Martin C. *The Problem of Democracy in Latin America*. Lexington, Mass.: Heath, 1987. A rebuttal of political culture interpretations of Latin American political reality.

———. *Mexican Politics*, 2nd ed. New York: Praeger, 1990. The most comprehensive recent treatment in English.

Neumann, Franz. *The Democratic and the Authoritarian State*. Glencoe, Ill.: Free Press, 1957. A great deal of wisdom on a variety of topics.

Norton, Philip. *The British Polity*. 2nd ed., New York: Longman, 1990. Norton comes closer than any other author of a general book on British politics to getting right all of the obscure precedents, implicit norms, and current practices.

Orwell, George (Eric Blair). *1984*. (various editions). An imaginative construction of a pure totalitarian system.

Rokkan, Stein. *Citizens, Elections, Parties*. New York: David McKay, 1970. Wide-ranging work whose core is a reinterpretation of European political history in the light of development theory.

Rose, Richard. "Class and Party Divisions: Britain as a Test Case," *Sociology*, May 1968. Seminal article by an author who has gone on to make a series of significant contributions.

Weber, Max. *Economy and Society*, Guenther Roth and Klaus Wittich, eds. New York: Bedminster Press, 1968. A three-volume display of erudition and intellectual power by a sociologist considered by many the greatest ever.

INDEX

heritage and, 73–74. *See also
names of specific countries*
Leeds, Anthony, 139
legitimacy: Africa and, 34; British prime minister and, 126;
defined, 33; of democracy, 30;
democratic, 32, 34; determining, 26–27; economy and, 60;
erosion of, 33; French president and, 125; government
stability and, 33–34; growth
of, 33; ideology and, 31; of
Juan Carlos, 28–29, 30; Latin
America and, 34; material interest and, 31; military rule
and, 59–60; monarchy and,
26, 28–31, 33; obedience and,
25, 33, 34; policy failure and,
33; religious, 32; revolutionary, 32–33; single-party government and, 59–60; Weber's
categorization of, 26, 31
Lenin, Vladimir, 20
Lerner, Daniel, 42
Lipset, Seymour Martin, 47–48
Lipson, Leslie, 98
Lleó, Manuel Urrutia, 8
Lueger, Karl, 7

MacMahon, Marshal, 125–26
Madero, Francisco, 9, 60
Mangin, William, 139
Marx, Karl, 5, 81
Marxism, 81, 141
Massachusetts Institute of Technology (M.I.T.), 40
Mexican Revolution, 4, 9–10, 60
Mexico, 60–64
Mexico City, 64
military rule, 57–60, 63, 113,
139–40
Mill, John Stuart, 21, 63
Mills, C. Wright, 107

Mitterrand, François, 129–30
modernization, 41–42, 43
monarchy: in Africa, 59; Britain
and, 51, 115, 118, 125; Germany and, 123; legitimacy
and, 26, 28–31, 33; in Spain,
27–28; succession and, 52;
U.S. Constitution and, 51
Morocco, 59
Muslim religion. *See* Islam
Mussolini, Benito, 14, 20

National University of Mexico,
63
*Nature of the Non-Western
World, The*, 41
Neumann, Franz, 20
New England, 74
Nicaragua, 114
1984, 13, 18, 20

Obregón, Alvaro, 9–10
O'Donnell, Guillermo, 41
Organski, Kenneth, 41
Orwell, George, 13

Pacific, South, 21
Paraguay, 22, 107
Party of National Action (PAN),
62
Perón, Juan, 16–17
Peru, 114, 130
Poland, 17, 19, 114, 130–31
political culture, 69–76
political development, economic
development and, 40, 41, 45
political development theory:
analytical approach to, 48; dependency theory of, 44–45;
economics and, 40; Frank and,
44; genesis of, 39–40; Huntington and, 43; Latin America and, 41, 43; modernization

ABOUT THE AUTHOR

MARTIN C. NEEDLER is dean of the School of International Studies at the University of the Pacific in Stockton, California. He has taught at the University of New Mexico, Dartmouth College, and the University of Michigan, and has held research appointments at Harvard and Oxford Universities and elsewhere. His articles have appeared in the journals of half a dozen countries and as many academic disciplines and in the Encyclopedia Americana. Dr. Needler is the author of *Mexican Politics: The Containment of Conflict*, 2nd ed. (Praeger, 1990).